THE ENCYCLOPEDIA OF

sharks

THE ENCYCLOPEDIA OF

sharks

STEVE AND JANE PARKER

APPLE

A QUINTET BOOK

Published by
The Apple Press
6 Blundell Street
London N7 9BH

ISBN 1-85076-860-9

This book was designed and produced by
Quintet Publishing Limited
6 Blundell Street
London N7 9BH

Creative Director: Richard Dewing
Art Director: Clare Reynolds
Designer: Simon Balley
Project Editor: Clare Hubbard
Editor: Andrew Armitage, MFE (Editorial Services)
Picture Research: Penni Bickle
Illustrator: Julian Baker

Typeset in Great Britain by
Central Southern Typesetters, Eastbourne

Manufactured in Singapore by
Bright Arts Pte Ltd

Printed in China by Leefung-Asco Printers Ltd

G 108176/5973
£16·99

Contents

title page: **A school of gray sharks swimming in the
waters off French Polynesia.**
left: **Symbol of strength, power, fear, and fury: the
great white, the world's largest predatory shark.**

CHAPTER 1

Talk About Sharks

Super-Killers!

A LONE TRIANGULAR-SHAPED FIN CUTS THE WATER'S SURFACE. SOMEONE ON THE BEACH NOTICES, AND YELLS: SHARK! BLIND PANIC AS PEOPLE SCREAM AND SCRAMBLE TO GET OUT OF THE WATER. ONE HOLIDAY-MAKER HAS DRIFTED SLIGHTLY OFFSHORE ON AN INFLATED RING.

He shouts and starts to kick the water. Then he yells in terror as the water boils for a few seconds … and he's gone. A stain of red appears at the surface and drifts slowly with the current. People on the beach stare horrified at his fate, but are so thankful it wasn't them.

This is the popular image of a shark—the mysterious, menacing, unstoppable, cold-blooded killer. It exists to seek out human prey, and strikes unseen from the dark depths, with unimaginable savagery. True, sharks are exciting, fascinating, and wondrously equipped hunters of the oceans. But most never contact humans. The movie-based image of all sharks as finned, bloodthirsty assassins is almost the exact opposite of the real picture.

habits and habitats

Sharks are highly adapted marine creatures, with types of behavior, bodily functions, and sensory powers we are only just beginning to understand. Their objectives are not to terrorize

right: **A real great white would never be so approachable! This fiber-glass model was used in the television series, Barrier Reef.**

previous page: **A curious great white cruises past the camera, mouth gaping to taste the water for traces of meat or blood.**

humans, but are much the same as any other living things, including ourselves. They try to feed, breed, and stay out of danger.

Depending on which shark expert you follow and how you classify sharks, there are between 375 and 475 different kinds, or species. Only 30 or so fit the typical stream-lined man-eater image. However, all sharks are built to a similar basic and very ancient design. It has been slightly altered here and there by millions of years of evolution, to produce creatures superbly adapted to many different ocean habitats—open water, weedy shallows, muddy dark depths, sandy or rocky coasts, and tropical, temperate, even polar temperatures.

stars of page and screen

Sharks are portrayed as savage killers in popular thriller novels and record-breaking films such as *Blue Water*, *White Death*, and the *Jaws* movies originating from the 1974 Peter Benchley book of the same name. Sharks also feature in *Moby Dick* by Herman Melville, Jules Verne's *20,000 Leagues Under The Sea*, and almost any other tale about sailors and seas.

The shark's terrible teeth are even mentioned in the Bible (Job 41:14). Some people believe that the "fish" or large marine animal that swallowed Jonah may, in fact, have been a huge shark, rather than a whale. The consequences of shark attack are vividly described in *The Threepenny Opera* by Bertolt Brecht, adapted for Frank Sinatra's hit song *Mac the Knife*: "When the shark bites, with his teeth, dear, scarlet billows start to spread."

beginning the redress

Publishers of the world's popular press indulge the general public's morbid fascination for blood and gore. Shark attacks fit the bill perfectly. However, accuracy was (and still is) usually sacrificed in favor of exaggerated savagery. At the turn of the century, the French magazine *Le Petit Parisien* reported that a shark

consumed an entire family—father, mother, child—at one sitting!

The French explorer and oceanographer Jacques Yves Cousteau (see page 28)—who died in mid-1997—helped to redress some of the balance. His splendid underwater films, photographs, commentaries, and books showed his sense of wonder and regard for these beautiful creatures, in perfect harmony with their natural world, swimming with power and grace. Many fascinating wildlife films and publications have continued these attempts to improve the shark's image, by being realistic and sensible, rather than sensational and emotional. This book is one of them.

above: **Safe shark-watching in a modern, hi-tech aquarium, where the fish live in relatively natural surroundings and viewers can study at their leisure.**

RECORD-BREAKERS

Record books are full of shark statistics. The largest of all the fish is the rare filter-feeding whale shark, while the largest predatory fish is the legendary great white shark. Sharks also feature heavily in the line-up of record-breaking angling catches (see page 21).

A Brief History of Sharks

COMPARED WITH THE TIME THAT SHARKS HAVE BEEN SWIMMING IN EARTH'S OCEANS—OVER 300 MILLION YEARS—OUR OWN RECORDED HISTORY IS A MERE BLINK OF THE EYE.

People have probably been aware of sharks, and the possibility of their attack, since humans began to swim or fish in the sea. Shark teeth and skins have been found at several Neolithic (New Stone Age) sites, including Maltese ruins occupied 4,000 years ago, when the dreaded great white shark was relatively common in the Mediterranean.

The first great scientific naturalist, Aristotle (384–322 BC) of Ancient Greece, traveled around the Mediterranean and studied its wildlife—especially marine creatures. In the manner of a conscientious biologist, he watched and observed and even dissected his subjects, in the quest for knowledge. His famous works include *The Parts of Animals*, *The Natural History of Animals* and *The Reproduction of Animals*.

Aristotle studied many kinds of fish, and he noted differences between fish in general and the various kinds of sharks. His observations included features such as the shark's lack of gill covers, its rough skin instead of true scales, a skeleton of cartilage (gristle) instead of true bone, bearing fully-developed young instead of laying tiny eggs, and certain differences of the internal organs. Modern biologists view these differences as fundamental in the evolution and classification of the animal kingdom.

that voracious fish

But Aristotle made errors. He mistakenly believed that the "claspers" of a male shark were used to hold the female during mating. He gave these organs their name, and it is still used, somewhat confusingly. "Old Ari" also thought the position of the shark mouth, some way back underneath the snout tip, made the shark turn upside-down to feed. He suggested that this maneuver gave prey a moment to escape. Otherwise, he believed, such a superb and insatiable predator would run out of victims, or gorge itself to death in the process.

Herodotus (485–425 BC), the Greek historian, set the trend for reporting gory shark attacks. He described the dreadful scene off Athos, northeast Greece, when many Persian boats sank during a sea battle, and their sailors were eaten

below: **Many older world maps portray fearsome creatures of the deep, including semi-realistic sharks and entirely mythical monsters.**

by sharks. In AD 77, the Roman naturalist Pliny the Elder reported attacks on sponge fishermen, as they climbed back into their boats with their harvest. In the sixteenth century, the French naturalist Guillame Rondelet described many examples of bodies that were removed whole from the stomachs of sharks—even a knight in a full suit of armor.

sharks on the rocks

In the seventeenth century, Niels Stenson (Nicolaus Steno) studied shark biology at the University of Copenhagen. Traveling around the Mediterranean, he came across "tongue-stones"—good-luck charms being sold in Malta. He recognized them as fossilized sharks' teeth. So the rocks of Malta, now an island, must once have been under the sea. A controversial idea indeed, for a time when the Bible's story of creation was taken literally.

From this notion, Stenson worked out that the deepest rocks must have been formed first. Known as the Principle of Superposition, or Steno's Law, this theory underlies most of modern geology.

above left: **The prospect of being devoured by sharks loomed large in the minds of tropical mariners—as it still does today.**

below: **A print from the early 1800s portrays the capture of basking sharks near the coast of Scotland. One carcass could feed a village and supply products for trade for weeks.**

Folk Tales With Teeth

AROUND THE WORLD, COASTAL PEOPLES HAVE TAKEN SHARKS INTO THEIR

MYTHS, FOLKLORES, LEGENDS, AND RELIGIONS (IF NOT INTO THEIR HEARTS!)

Those who depended on fishing and sailing were only too aware of the dangers of the deep—especially sharks.

Some responded by worshipping the sharks as gods, who would hopefully be appeased by ceremonies and even sacrifices, and perhaps protect the boats and make catches more bountiful. Other people took a different route, chased and caught sharks, and subjected them to cruel tortures.

european hatred

Sharks have long been hated by European mariners, not only because they occasionally attacked people, but because they were held responsible for small fish yields.

Catching a shark was considered good luck, especially if it was a pregnant female—fewer sharks in the sea! The unfortunate shark was dis-emboweled and its tail cut off, being nailed to the ship's bowsprit as a good-luck trophy. The shark itself, probably still alive, was thrown back into the sea, to a chorus of satisfied jeers.

Some sailors believed that sharks could smell a corpse on board, and they would follow the ship relentlessly, until the body was committed to the deep—burial at sea. As a consequence, many Europeans refused to eat shark meat, since it could be "recycled" human flesh. Many reports of shark stomach contents encouraged this belief.

the new world and the east

On the other side of the Atlantic, the pirate-ridden Caribbean of the nineteenth century was home to two legendary man-eating sharks. "Port Royal Jack" was a large great white who lazily

right: **Greenland sharks are a type of sleeper shark. They feed voraciously on offal from fish-processing ships and coastal stations, earning them the name of gurry sharks.**

TALK ABOUT SHARKS

left: **This body paint of Pacific Islanders, used in traditional dances, represents the stripes of a deadly sea snake. It may also help to deter shark attacks.**

below: **The yellowfin tuna, a regular prey of larger oceanic sharks, and occasionally itself mistaken for a shark.**

patrolled the harbor entrance at Kingston, Jamaica, waiting for his next meal to fall in, probably in a drunken stupor. "Shanghai Bill" indulged in the same habits off Bridgetown, Barbados. He reputedly died choking on the shaggy coat of a large dog who went for a swim.

In Ancient Japan there were many gods—including a shark. He was god of storms, and his image symbolized fear. Even today, Japanese fishermen believe that wearing a long red sash protects against sharks. Along Vietnam's coasts are ancient shrines, apparently dedicated to the mighty whale shark.

The pearl divers of the East descend to amazing depths in the water, holding their breath for two or three minutes and enduring great pressures. They were exposed to another danger as they were struggling back into their boats—the menace of sharks. In Ceylon (now Sri Lanka), the divers employed snake-charmers to adapt their technique and to subdue the marauding fish.

More Toothy Tales

MANY MYTHICAL TALES AND STORIES ABOUT THE SHARK ORIGINATE FROM THE ISLANDS OF THE GREAT PACIFIC OCEAN, WHICH COVERS ALMOST HALF THE GLOBE.

above: **Human skulls probably damaged as a result of a shark attack, perhaps as the result of deliberate sacrifice by their fellow villagers.**

above right: **In a shark-aware region, any pointed prominence lends itself to decoration, like these rocks bordering a coastal highway in California.**

As ancient peoples "island-hopped" in their eastward migrations across the Pacific Ocean, they took their traditions with them. Unique cultures developed on each island group, and the much-feared shark featured strongly in many of these beliefs and traditions.

New Guinea Islanders and Polynesians had great respect for the shark. They believed it could exert terrible magic, and so it must never be caught or harmed in any way.

For Solomon Islanders, sharks were believed to be incarnations of the spirits of dead ancestors. These spirits needed appeasing, so they would protect the community. Therefore the sharks must be fed on meat—often human meat. With great ingenuity, the islanders built underwater altars near the caves where these spirit-sharks were thought to live, and sacrificed "volunteers" there.

the shark king

In Hawaii, the king of the sharks was Kamo Hoa Lii. He lived near Honolulu, while his shark queen, Oahu, lived in what is now Pearl Harbor. In ancient times, the Hawaiian people built large stone pens on the sea bed. Within a pen, young warriors armed only with sticks proved their worth by wrestling the all-too-real "subjects" of the legendary shark king. If they failed, they were sacrificed to Kamo Hoa Lii.

Hawaiian traditions tell the story of the mischievous demigod Maui. He was insulted by a shark while fishing, so he grabbed the shark and hurled it far into the sky. It can still be seen there, as star patterns within the Milky Way. Another shark managed to escape from the fishing hook of Maui and swam away, to become the island of Tahiti.

kissing sharks?

Some Pacific Islanders had shark totems, individual fish living wild, but marked with tar. In a shallow bay, the priest would summon this totem fish with rattles and feed on entrails. The shark cruised around the priest's canoe, while he stroked it and muttered prayers, believing the shark would become harmless.

Other islanders in the Pacific believed that kissing a shark rendered it harmless. To this end, kissing ceremonies were performed regularly. The human participants included in this ritual prepared for their ordeal by taking kava, a plant extract with narcotic effects. Often, the shark did become harmless—too full of food to threaten anyone else.

below: **This varnished driftwood carving from the South Pacific Pitcairn Islands is decorated with real shark's teeth.**

DECORATIVE SHARKS

Peoples of the Pacific and other oceanic areas have used sharks' teeth for ceremonial necklaces, bracelets, and ear decorations, and also to tip their daggers, spears and other weapons. The traditions continue today, and souvenir stores in tropical holiday resorts bristle with sharks' teeth jewelry, whole jaws as trophies, and even walking sticks made from the dried, gristle-like backbones.

Even Sharks Have Uses

THE MOST OBVIOUS USE FOR SHARKS IS MEAT TO EAT. MOST TYPES OF SHARK FLESH ARE EDIBLE, INDEED, SOME ARE VERY TASTY, AND POPULAR AROUND THE WORLD.

above: **A small specimen of the mackerel shark group is offered for sale at Bombay fish market, India.**

right: **Throughout the Far East, shark fins are regarded as a tasty delicacy and are believed to possess medicinal and healing powers.**

Shark steaks are a daily staple food in parts of the Pacific, yet they also feature increasingly on restaurant menus in Western cities, often as an exotic and expensive treat. For conservative diners wary of new trends, the names may be changed. For example, the meat of the small shark called the dogfish is variously termed rock salmon, rock eel, huss, or flake.

In many Eastern regions, such as China and Japan, shark flesh is eaten in various forms, fresh or dried or even raw. There are shark fillets, steaks, fishcakes, sharkburgers, fishpastes, and, of course, shark's-fin soup. The fins of several species can be used, but the most famous is the tope, the soupfin shark. This shark probably got its name because it is the easiest shark to catch and is commonly found off the coast of California where the shark meat would be sold in the restaurants in China Town. Traditionally the fins are cut off, dusted with salt or lime, sun-dried, and processed into dried fibrous disks. These dissolve when boiled to produce a fish-flavored, gelatinous soup.

If a shark's flesh is not considered good enough for the meat market, it can be rendered down, together with leftover entrails and other parts, to produce fish oil and meal for animal feed or fertilizer.

shark-liver oil

For its body size, a shark has an enormous liver. For example, a porbeagle shark 10 feet long yields around 1¼ gallons of liver oil. A big basking shark could produce about 5,300. The liver and its oil are rich sources of minerals and vitamins, especially vitamin E. The oil is also used in cosmetics, paints, lubricants, candles, lighting fuel, and leather-tanning. Hammerhead oil is particularly high-quality. Baby sharks developing inside their mother yield a similar rich, oily fluid.

The shark-liver industry was once substantial. During the early twentieth century, Scandinavians caught 30,000 or more Greenland sharks yearly. Cheaper synthetic alternatives mean that this trade has largely disappeared in the West. But in the East, people still seek the benefits of shark-liver oil.

One of its ingredients, squalene, is purified and sold in capsules as a cure-all health tonic. Squalene has also been used to treat burns, and as a base for cosmetics. Reputedly, the liver oil became an engine lubricant in Japanese aircraft during World War Two.

shark skin

Shark skin was once a sought-after product—tough, stronger than cowhide, flexible, often attractively marked. Removed from the carcass, trimmed, soaked in brine for several weeks, and treated, it becomes shagreen. This still bears the tiny, pointed, toothlike "scales," dermal denticles, and was used as an abrasive by carpenters, metal-workers, and jewelers, for smoothing and polishing. It also served as a grip for swords and daggers—non-slip even when blood-soaked—and as a novelty covering for books, cigarette lighters, and trinkets.

Tope, carpet sharks, zebra sharks, and darkie-charlies made the best shagreen.

Tanning shark skin removes the denticles to produce a soft leather for shoes, purses, brief-cases, and books. Nurse, tiger, silky, carpet, and lemon sharks all have beautiful markings that made them targets for the shark leather trade. This is now controlled by conservation laws.

below: **Shark products continue to enjoy a reputation as an aid to human health. After all, few people have seen a sickly shark.**

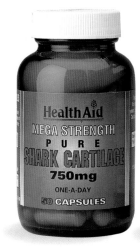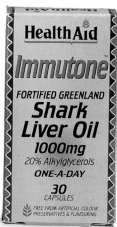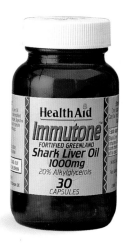

SHARK-BASED MEDICINES

Traditional treatments for human ailments, using parts of sharks, are many and varied. Whether they really work is the subject of ongoing medical research (see page 32).

- Shark's bile or gall-bladder extract for eye cataracts.
- Baked shark ashes for teething pains and ringworm.
- Dried shark brain to prevent dental decay and ease labor pains.
- Powdered sharks' teeth for gallstones and excessive bleeding.

Who's Afraid of Sharks?

MOST PEOPLE SEEM TO HAVE AN INNATE OR BUILT-IN FEAR OF SHARKS, AS OF SPIDERS AND SNAKES. BUT WHY? PROBABLY BECAUSE THEY ARE BEYOND OUR EXPERIENCE AND UNDERSTANDING.

Few people ever actually encounter a real shark, other than perhaps safely behind aquarium glass. Our fear and terror of sharks probably stems from several roots based in our primeval psyche, but little factual information or realistic common sense.

Sharks have probably received bad press from the beginnings of storytelling and written history. Around ancient seaside campfires, people may well have retold and embellished tales of "horrific" shark attacks. They knew only about the sharks who inflicted terrible wounds on sailors, fishermen, and divers. The vast majority of sharks went unseen and harmlessly about their business.

Dread of sharks may also come from sub-conscious fears of the unknown and the unexpected. Many people, and animals, have an instinctive fear of water, especially deeper water. Who knows what might be hiding there? If there is a shark, it may well strike swiftly and without warning. The victim can rarely see it coming.

no expression, no emotion

The appearance of a shark is also very worrying to us. People communicate by facial expressions and bodily gestures, showing intelligence and emotions. But a shark seems to move mechanically, like a robot. It has hard and rough skin, a totally expressionless face, and glassy staring eyes—not unlike a snake. It is apparently without feelings, compassion, reason, even consciousness. This lack of responsive psychology is profoundly unsettling for most people.

People who try to study, experience, and understand sharks often quickly come to admire their sleek, sensuous grace, their fascinating behavior, and their incredible array of senses. Patient scientific observation is revealing not moronic robots, but creatures who are aware of each other and of other creatures, who communicate and work together, who can learn, and who even indulge in behavior we might term "play." Some sharks undoubtedly attack people—but we could be viewed as threatening invaders in their world.

below: **A shark's eye view of a crowded bathing beach, with its all-action ripples, splashes, and cloudy water.**

left: **Lest they forget—signs warn bathers near the Captain Cook Bridge, Botany Bay, Australia.**

Catching Sharks

THERE ARE PERHAPS **20** REPORTED SHARK ATTACKS EACH YEAR WHICH RESULT IN HUMAN FATALITIES. THAT'S ABOUT ONE TON OF PEOPLE.

Meanwhile humans catch and kill more than 77,000 tons of sharks, and their close relatives the skates and rays, yearly (see page 32). This includes commercial fishing by large boats for profit, local and traditional fishing for mainly domestic needs, and angling as a sport.

shark fisheries

Commercial fishing for sharks has some, but limited, success. Sharks breed relatively slowly, so local stocks are soon wiped out by modern, efficient boats. Smaller-scale, opportunistic pursuit of individually valuable fish is usually more productive.

above: **A hammerhead shark landed on the beach at New Caledonia, in the south-west Pacific. For local people, it could mean a human life saved.**

right: **A New Zealand fisherman proudly displays a mako shark, one of the fastest and potentially more dangerous species.**

However, some sharks support a regular trade. The dogfish, also known as the rough hound or lesser spotted dogfish, is common in European waters, from the Shetland Islands south to the Mediterranean. Popular for fish dishes, several thousand tons are caught by trawlers every year.

Another North Atlantic commercial target is the spiny dogfish, or spurdog. Some 55,000 tons are taken from around the coast of Britain alone every year. But this species does not breed until at least five years of age, so the replacement rate is low. Continued fishing at this level could wipe them out.

A few other species are caught commercially around the world. Soupfin sharks supply the Chinese food market and threshers are still caught in numbers, for food and oil production.

a sporting chance?

Sports angling is big business, and may be affecting the populations of some sharks, particularly the great white. Even if the sharks themselves are not hooked, commercial fishing boats are catching many other kinds of fish for human consumption, thus depriving the sharks of food. Certain people like to demonstrate their dominance over the supposed "terror of the deep," with ever more sophisticated methods of catching and killing their trophies.

Not surprisingly, very large specimens have become hard to find. To qualify for a record-breaking catch, the angler must have no help from anyone else until the fish is alongside the boat or shore, and the line must never touch any part of the boat or shore.

The mako is a favorite sports fish because it puts up a long, spirited, and spectacular fight, leaping repeatedly from the water. The great white is less exciting since it dives to deeper water when hooked, and uses sheer strength.

In British waters, the blue shark is popular with sea anglers. But it's less so with trawler crews, who say that these sharks attack their catches and cause damage to the nets.

RECORD-BREAKERS

The largest fish ever caught on rod and line was a great white shark, 16·8 feet long and weighing just over a ton—or 2,664 pounds—in Australia in 1959. (A large adult human averages 176 pounds.)

- A bigger great white of 3,389 pounds was landed in 1976 but the equipment and methods used to catch it meant that it did not qualify for the record books.
- A massive great white, a little over 20 feet long and weighing 5,000 pounds, was caught off the Azores in 1978, but by harpoon, not rod and line.
- Other international record-breaking shark catches include a hammerhead of 991 pounds, a porbeagle of 507 pounds, and a thresher of 802 pounds.

above: **A scalloped hammerhead is hauled aboard by sports anglers off of the coast of Florida.**

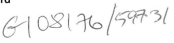

MANY PEOPLE ARE KILLED OR INJURED EVERY YEAR BY ALL MANNER OF ANIMALS. MARINE DANGERS INCLUDE CERTAIN JELLYFISH, BOX-JELLIES AND SEA-WASPS, BLUE-RINGED OCTOPUSES, STONEFISH AND LIONFISH, SEA SNAKES, AND SALTWATER CROCODILES.

In terms of numbers of people suffering, sharks are near the bottom of this list. People are far more likely to win a national lottery, or die in an automobile accident, than be attacked by a shark!

True, shark attacks seem to be rising. But this is probably not due to their increased ferocity and cunning. Likely causes are more reporting of attacks compared with previous years, and more people in the sea. A catalog of recorded shark attacks could fill this book. Some of the more significant ones are described on pages 26–27.

the threat in perspective

About 80 percent of shark attack victims survive. Often, the shark is carrying out only an "exploratory" assault, as explained below. Of the hundred or so reported attacks worldwide each year, usually fewer than 20 of these cases are fatal. Bee stings kill more people annually in the United States alone.

above: **From below, the silhouette of a surfer on a board may be similar enough to the outline of a seal, for a shark to attack.**

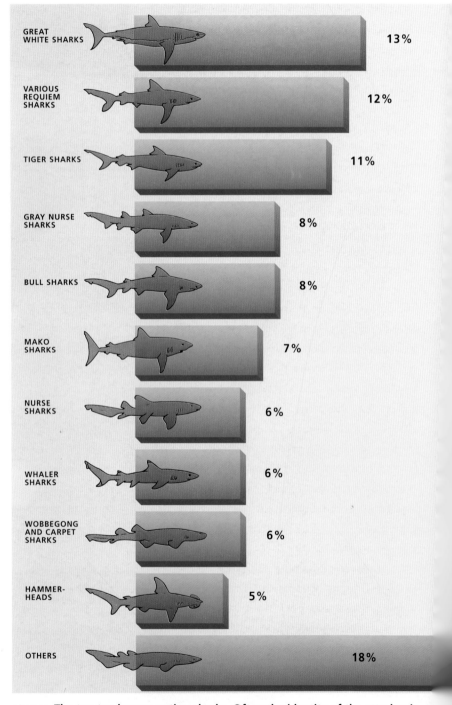

GREAT WHITE SHARKS	13%
VARIOUS REQUIEM SHARKS	12%
TIGER SHARKS	11%
GRAY NURSE SHARKS	8%
BULL SHARKS	8%
MAKO SHARKS	7%
NURSE SHARKS	6%
WHALER SHARKS	6%
WOBBEGONG AND CARPET SHARKS	6%
HAMMER-HEADS	5%
OTHERS	18%

above: **The top ten human-eating sharks. Often the identity of the attacker is not certain, but bite marks can sometimes be a clue.**

Globally, people are almost 1,000 times more likely to drown than be attacked by a shark. Even in Australia, where sharks and people in the sea are relatively common, drownings outnumber shark attacks by fifty to one.

Most reported attacks occur in warm, calm, shallow waters near tropical holiday resorts. They happen more frequently during weekends, and usually in the afternoon. The victims tend to be affluent Westerners. These statistics reflect people's vacation habits and global tourism, rather than the behavior of sharks. Attacks on poorer people along the coasts of poorer countries may well go unrecorded.

a result of instinct

Like most wild creatures in their natural habitats, sharks are usually on the lookout for food. Big sharks, such as great whites, feed on correspondingly big prey, such as seals and sea lions. Injured individuals, who cannot swim properly, make especially attractive targets for any predator. So when a shark picks up the sounds, waterborne scents, and vibrations of a large mammal, thrashing at the sea's surface, their instinct is to investigate a potential meal.

Many reports of attacks on humans describe the shark coming in first for an investigatory nudge or two. It may well then disappear, choosing to avoid this unfamiliar creature. If it follows up with an attack, the initial bite may also be cautious and exploratory, since most sharks have never encountered human flesh before. Occasionally, however, the shark charges fast and bites hard first time. Then, following a feeding behavior honed by millions of years of evolution, in which there were no humans, it may continue to bite and swallow the victim while ignoring rescuers who come to help.

above:

Most feared attacker, the great white.

below:

Shark expert Rod Fox displays his own scars and a shark who suffered far more.

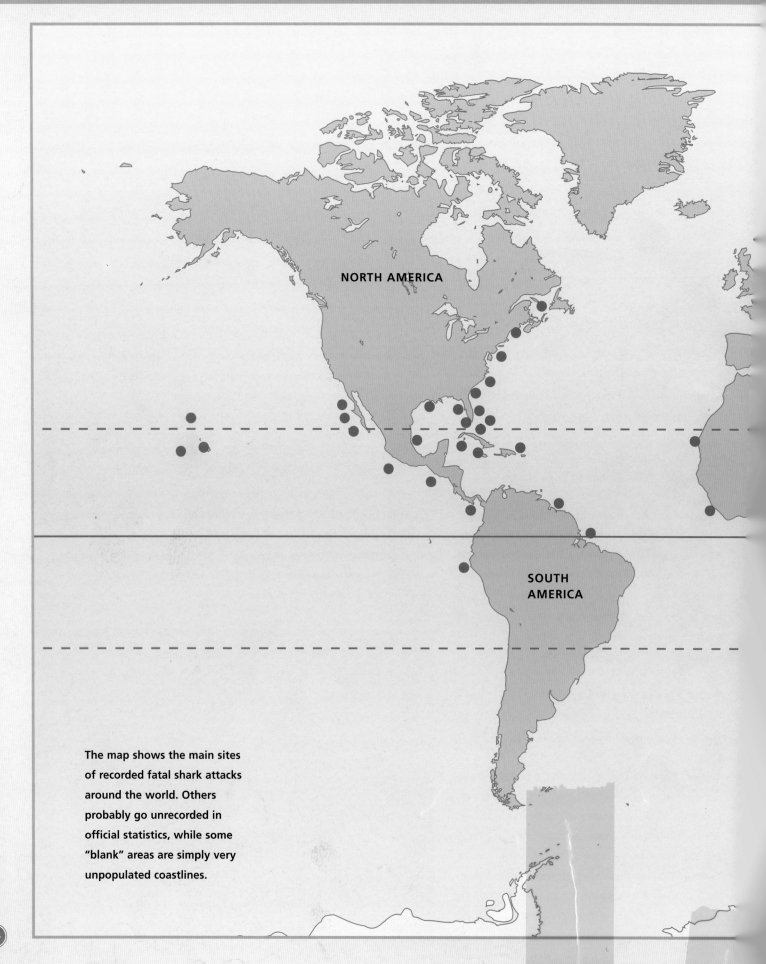

NORTH AMERICA

SOUTH AMERICA

The map shows the main sites
of recorded fatal shark attacks
around the world. Others
probably go unrecorded in
official statistics, while some
"blank" areas are simply very
unpopulated coastlines.

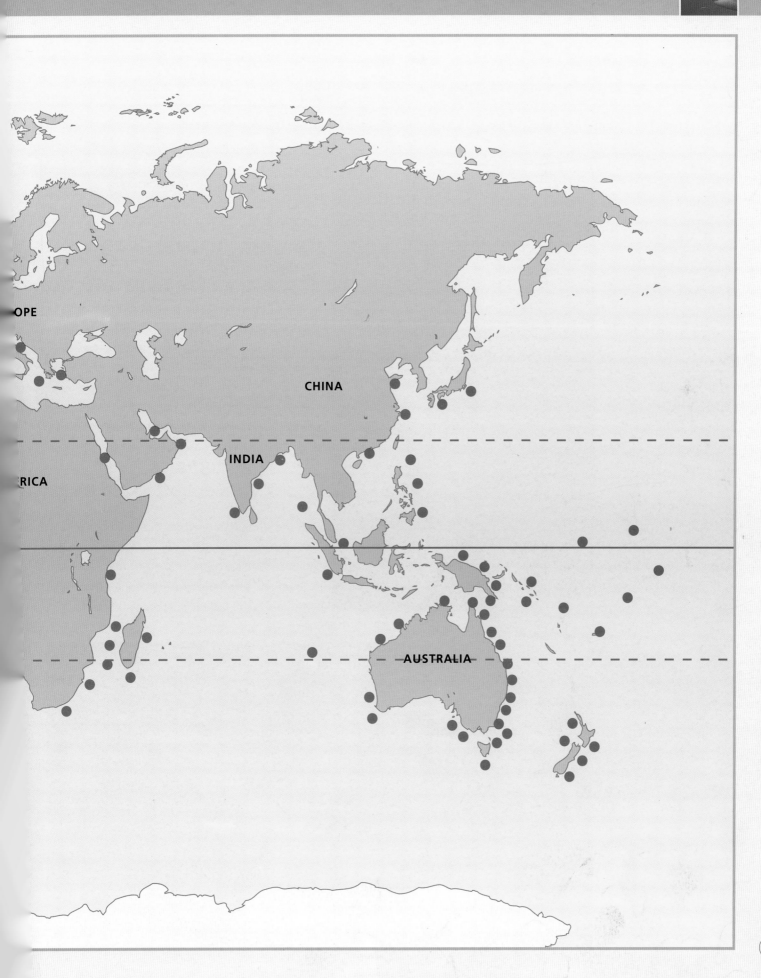

OPE

RICA

CHINA

INDIA

AUSTRALIA

Sharks in War

ONE OF THE FIRST INCIDENTS OF A SHARK ATTACK RECORDED FOR POSTERITY WAS IN **1580**.

A SEAMAN FELL OVERBOARD ON A VOYAGE FROM PORTUGAL TO INDIA.

right: **The swift and agile mako (also called the shortfin mako), has a reputation for the un-warned sudden strike.**

below: **The tiger shark, large and powerful, has an unstoppable final surge.**

As his shipmates tried to pull him back with a line, he was suddenly torn apart. The account of the tragedy whetted the public appetite for shark-related blood and gore, and reports have flowed ever since.

In World War Two, the problem of shark attack threatened the morale of Navy and Air Force personnel from various nations. In 1942 a German U-boat holed the Allied steamer *Nova Scotia* off South Africa. The ship sank in minutes, leaving 900 men in the water. By the time a rescue ship arrived 60 hours later, there were only 192 survivors, owing to a gathering of sharks.

the *indianapolis* tragedy

In 1945 the USS *Indianapolis* was torpedoed by a Japanese submarine. The cruiser was returning to the United States from the Tinian air base in the Pacific, after delivering parts of the atomic bomb to be dropped on Hiroshima. It went down and left more than 1,000 men floating in the sea, in life jackets or clinging to wreckage.

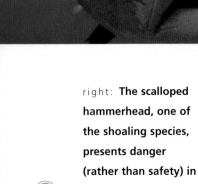

right: **The scalloped hammerhead, one of the shoaling species, presents danger (rather than safety) in numbers.**

EVEN DEAD SHARKS BITE

In 1977 Mark Green was driving home with a dead shark in the car, which he had caught while fishing. He was involved in an accident, was flung on to the shark's teeth, and needed 22 stitches in his resulting wounds!

Owing to the secrecy of the atomic bomb mission, the loss of the Indianapolis was not acted upon until three days later. On the fourth day, rescuers arrived to find 883 men missing—most killed by sharks in front of their surviving shipmates.

In response, the United States Navy issued its *Shark Sense* manual, a step-by-step guide to avoid being eaten. This assured worried readers that a shark could not see and bite at the same time. So the recommended actions were:

Step 1 Make a quick sideways lunge as the shark bites, so it misses its target

Step 2 Catch hold of the dorsal fin as the shark charges past

Step 3 To stay out of harm's way, hold onto the fin for as long as possible, without drowning!

the most feared sharks

The most feared sharks, known to attack humans, include the great white (man-eater, white pointer, or whaler), tiger shark, hammerhead, mako (blue pointer), bronze and blacktipped whalers, and the oceanic white-tip.

The bull shark is also extremely dangerous. Although not internationally infamous, it is number three on the killer list after the great white and the tiger shark. But others, even the normally inoffensive wobbegong, may attack in self-defense and easily remove a hand or foot.

Sharks live the single life. They usually swim, attack, and feed alone. But lots of bodies and blood in the water attract them from a huge area, so this is why they seem to be attacking in shoals.

There are occasional stories of sharks who develop a taste for human flesh, like a man-eating tiger or lion. In Queensland, Australia, in 1983, three people were left in the water when their boat sank. They were picked off one by one by the same shark.

above: **The USS *Indianapolis*.**

above left: **The copper shark, also known around Australia as the bronze whaler, and around the United States as the narrowtooth shark, has been implicated in various attacks.**

TALK ABOUT SHARKS

27

Sharks and Science

above: **A great white checks out divers in a metal cage, while they do the reverse, observing and photographing its behavior.**

and scientists, he carried out much original research in the 1950s and 1960s. Cousteau was struck by the "murderous yet beautiful force" of these "splendid savages of the sea." He helped to design the first SCUBA (Self-Contained Underwater Breathing Apparatus) equipment and pioneered the use of shark cages for observation and filming.

Today, successful film-makers such as Ron and Valerie Taylor continue these valuable observations on sharks. They use chain-mail suits for protection as they dive among their subjects.

contributions to education

The dogfish, a small species of shark, has taught generations of young scientists about fish biology. Easy to keep and breed in cold-water aquaria, they are an ideal sea-fish version of the laboratory rat, for dissection and study. Dogfish research has also produced significant information about the finely tuned senses of sharks, their swimming prowess, their physiology (body chemistry and functions) and the way they breed. The recent trend to large sea-life centers is helping this work.

The best place to study sharks is to be among them, in their natural marine habitat. Advances in diving and camera technology make this increasingly rewarding.

Work around islands off the coast of California shows the behavior of great white sharks, using remote-controlled underwater cameras on the ends of long poles. The "Crittercam," a small camera attached to a shark, records the shark's view as it swims. The strap that holds the camera disintegrates after two hours, when the camera floats to the surface, emits a radio signal, and is recovered.

Serious science eats up money, and serious money is usually available only for research that might lead to useful applications and profits. Academic research into sharks for their own sake is more difficult to fund.

Shark scientists work mainly in three overlapping and potentially profitable fields. These are finding suitable shark deterrents, developing useful shark products, and unraveling the biology and ecology of commercially fished sharks.

for the sake of knowledge

One of the first people to attempt serious underwater studies of sharks was the late Jacques Yves Cousteau (see page 9). With his teams of underwater photographers, film-makers, explorers,

left: **A whitetip reef shark tests the lightweight mesh suit of shark photographer and expert Valerie Taylor.**

above: **A juvenile hammerhead shark is force-fed a tracking device that will beam out radio signals, allowing researchers to follow it for several days.**

Deterrents and Death

MANY SCIENTIFIC STUDIES ON SHARKS AIM TO MAKE OCEAN BATHING AND SWIMMING SAFER FOR US, BY SOMEHOW REPELLING OR DETERRING THEM— HOPEFULLY IN A HUMANE AND ENLIGHTENED FASHION.

The United States Navy commissioned shark biologists for the first full-scale study of shark-repelling methods, during World War Two. They took as their laboratory "model" the test of keeping dogfish, that small and useful shark, away from fresh meat.

The scientists tried sounds of various pitches, poisons, and irritants that worked on other fish, nasty waterborne scents, even toxic gases. Only one chemical seemed to have any effect—copper acetate. Bottled as Shark Chaser, it was issued to all military personnel at sea. It may have boosted morale, but it was probably virtually useless to shipwrecked sailors and underwater divers. More recent tests show that it may even have attracted sharks!

understanding the deterrent

Gradually scientists realized that, to find a shark deterrent, they needed to understand sharks better. The first scientific meeting about sharks, where researchers discussed their work and results, was held in 1954.

In the 1990s, after much further research, the range of repellents or deterrents is less than impressive, and not even fully proven in most situations:

• Large, floating, black plastic bags which disguise the victim's shape and prevent body fluids leaking into the sea

• Electric-field generators which upset a shark's senses

• The chemical tardaxin, given off by certain flatfish (the moses sole) to prevent sharks eating them

• Black and white striped wet suits that confuse the shark's sensitivity to contrasting shapes

to kill a shark

Another approach is to kill marauding sharks. But this is amazingly difficult. Sports anglers are resigned to clubbing, hacking, and even shooting their catches repeatedly. A shark may try to

right: **Confuse-a-shark? This underwater umbrella, like several of the visual devices under test for distracting or deterring shark attacks, has a pattern of bold stripes.**

above: **This sand tiger shark was finally dispatched by the "power-head" electric stun device.**

above right: **Testing repellers like this electrical version is a hazardous task, especially against great whites.**

IF MENACED BY A SHARK

People who survive shark attacks advise the following:

• Avoid risky locations—swim within a shark protection zone

• If a shark appears, swim quickly, quietly, powerfully, and smoothly, away from the area

• Avoid splashing and erratic or uncoordinated movements

• Remain under the surface for as long as possible

• If a shark does attack, a punch to its snout, eyes, or gills may be effective (then again, it may not …)

struggle and bite, even an hour after being dragged from the water. The shark's survival powers are admirably awesome.

In one experiment, sharks were injected with very large doses of poison, normally lethal to similarly large animals. The effects were minimal. Of 30 poisons tested, strychnine was the only type effective against large sharks. But it took eight minutes to work—too long in an attack situation.

There is still no completely effective way of protecting humans from sharks. Resort beaches depend on physical barriers made of bars or chain-link fencing, plus lookouts in high towers or spotter planes. Individual divers may carry electric stun-prods. The latest protection device developed by South African scientists is a "wand" called POD which produces a weak electric shock (rather than a stunning device which could shock the diver) and interferes with the shark's electro-reception system. Gill-nets are regularly used on popular beaches, to catch any sharks that have penetrated the barriers. This practice however, is very controversial because other marine creatures, such as dolphins and turtles can become trapped in the nets.

Future Uses for Sharks

AS TRADITIONALLY CAUGHT FOOD SPECIES OF FISH BECOME MORE SCARCE,

COMMERCIAL FISHING TURNS TO SHARKS.

Many environmental and conservation bodies, even the United Nations, worry that the sharks' slow reproductive rate may not be able to cope.

We do not know the short- or long-term effects on the ocean ecosystems of losing these top predators. More research into shark populations and ecology would help to fix realistic world quotas for shark fishing.

shark medicines

Eastern systems of medicine have long looked to animals as sources of potions to cure all manner of ailments. Most of these substances remain untried by Western scientific medicine. Some have been investigated, but proved ineffective.

However, this does not mean that sharks cannot benefit human health in the future.

Sharks seem astonishingly free of normal forms of illness and disease. Very few of the thousands of sharks caught appear to suffer from cancer, bacterial infections, or other disorders. The shark's immune system may provide some clues.

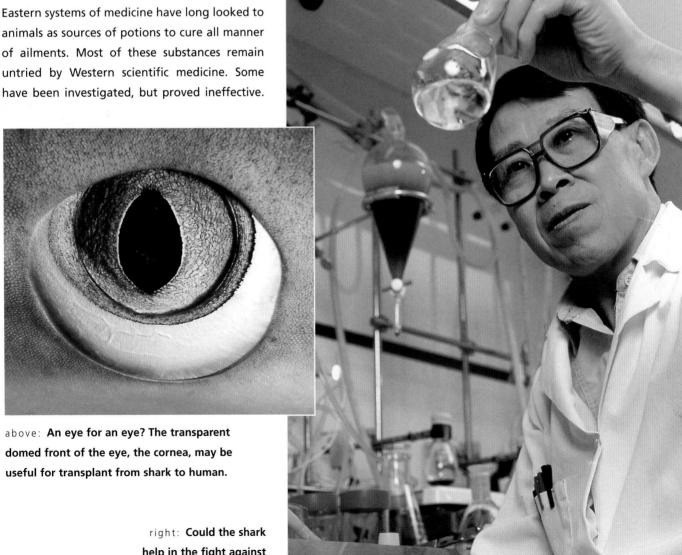

above: **An eye for an eye? The transparent domed front of the eye, the cornea, may be useful for transplant from shark to human.**

right: **Could the shark help in the fight against human disease?**

above: **Squalamine and similar shark-derived chemicals may be potential antibiotic drugs, able to kill bacteria which have become resistant to our normal antiobiotic agents.**

a miracle cure?

Researchers from the United States have tested a natural chemical called squalamine, extracted from dogfish, to see if it is effective at killing bacterial microbes and so treating certain infectious diseases. Squalamine is also being studied for its possible uses in killing body cells which have become infected with disease-causing viral microbes, and in removing potential tumor cells by preventing the growth from developing its own blood supply. Shark blood is known to contain an anticoagulant, or anti-blood-clotting chemical, which may have a use in treating patients suffering from certain forms of heart disease. Such potential medical uses are the subject of ongoing research.

Many well-established medicinal substances are made from shark cartilage (the skeletal framework), including a burns treatment. Shark tissues such as the cornea of the eye may even be useful for human transplants.

Much of this work is at an early stage. But, like yet undiscovered substances in tropical rain-forests, shark products could yield useful drugs and medications in the fight against human disease and suffering.

CHAPTER 2
Shark Success

Survival of the Fittest

THE FORCES AND EFFECTS OF EVOLUTION BY NATURAL SELECTION HAVE SHAPED AND ALTERED ALL ASPECTS OF LIVING THINGS—INCLUDING SHARKS.

PRIMITIVE OR ADVANCED?

Sharks appeared over 300 million years ago, as shown by the fossil record. Their basic form has remained largely unchanged through all this time. But this does not mean they are "primitive." Today's sharks have not stopped evolving. They are bang up to date and ideally suited for present-day environments. Nature came up with a good fundamental design at a very early stage.

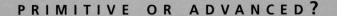

above: **The basic shark design has remained remarkably stable since it first evolved.** *Cladoselache* (above) **swam in the seas 350 million years before the very similar dogfish (below).**

This is encapsulated by the phrase "survival of the fittest." Every generation of life forms contains variations of many kinds, in size, shape, strength, body chemistry, behavioral patterns, and hundreds of other factors.

Much of the variation is due to the individual's unique genetic make-up, inherited from its parents. Other variations come from the effects of the environment, such as eating different types and amounts of foods, or being exposed to different physical conditions and dangers.

sharks are individuals, too

We recognize individuality in ourselves so easily. We all have our individual traits and personal histories. Unlikely as it may seem, no two sharks are identical, either. They are all individuals. Some of the differences are subtle and hardly obvious to us: perhaps a slightly smoother outline shape, or skin of a fractionally darker shade. Other variations are more dramatic, such as extra teeth, or an oddly shaped fin.

Among this range of different individuals, some are better adapted or suited to cope with the demands of their surroundings and the challenges of life. They may be slightly more powerful swimmers, or their skin coloring provides marginally improved camouflage.

These "fitter" animals are more likely to survive and breed successfully. They pass on their genes to the next generation, in preference to those who cope less well. Gradually, by the selecting forces of nature, they evolve.

previous page: **Gray reef sharks whirl and twist in a graceful underwater ballet.**

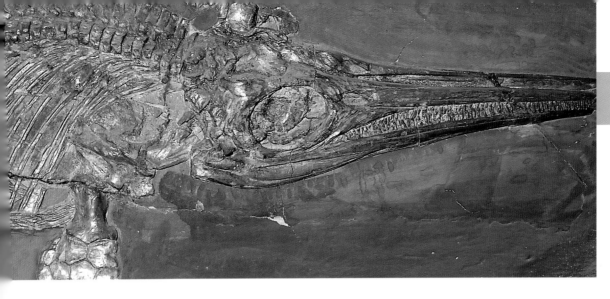

left: **Ichthyosaurs were sea-going and shark-shaped, but were reptiles from the Dinosaur Age.**

the never-ending chase

This is how sharks first appeared, and how the different species have adapted to different surroundings or habitats. But it is a never-ending process. The world's climate changes gradually, over millions of years, with ice ages, droughts, and heatwaves. Other living things evolve too, like prey and competitors, and they make up part of the surroundings. It's a never-ending process as animals and plants struggle to keep ahead of the game.

But survival is always a compromise. No living thing is perfectly suited to all environments and eventualities. For example, many sharks are excellent at swimming fast forwards. But the adaptations for this, including rigid fins and a relatively inflexible body, mean that they are poor at maneuvering in small spaces. Sharks cannot stop suddenly or swim backwards, like many other fish. Sometimes, they swim onward into danger.

similar designs

The process of evolution has produced similar solutions to a problem, from different starting points. The prehistoric reptile called the ichthyosaur, and today's dolphin, tuna, and great white shark, all have the same basic body outline. These animals are not similar due to close relationships, but to similar lifestyles. Nature has shaped them all to move swiftly and powerfully through the water as fast-swimming, ocean-going hunters. It's called convergent evolution, and there are many examples between the shark and other sea creatures.

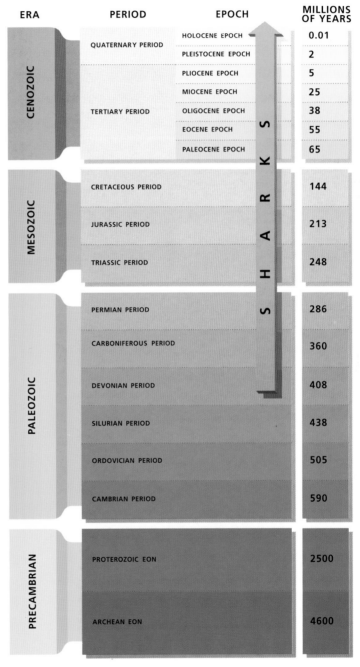

ERA	PERIOD	EPOCH	MILLIONS OF YEARS
CENOZOIC	QUATERNARY PERIOD	HOLOCENE EPOCH	0.01
		PLEISTOCENE EPOCH	2
		PLIOCENE EPOCH	5
	TERTIARY PERIOD	MIOCENE EPOCH	25
		OLIGOCENE EPOCH	38
		EOCENE EPOCH	55
		PALEOCENE EPOCH	65
MESOZOIC	CRETACEOUS PERIOD		144
	JURASSIC PERIOD		213
	TRIASSIC PERIOD		248
PALEOZOIC	PERMIAN PERIOD		286
	CARBONIFEROUS PERIOD		360
	DEVONIAN PERIOD		408
	SILURIAN PERIOD		438
	ORDOVICIAN PERIOD		505
	CAMBRIAN PERIOD		590
PRECAMBRIAN	PROTEROZOIC EON		2500
	ARCHEAN EON		4600

right: **Earth's prehistory is divided into eras, which are divided into periods, named for the rocks that were laid down at that time. Fossils can be dated by the type of rock in which they are found. Fossils in Precambrian rocks are very rare. The fossil record of sharks begins in Devonian rocks.**

Records in the Rocks

SCIENTISTS WHO STUDY PAST LIFE ARE CALLED PALEONTOLOGISTS. THEY SPEND MUCH TIME LOOKING AT FOSSILS—THE REMAINS OF PLANTS, ANIMALS, AND OTHER ONCE-LIVING THINGS, PRESERVED IN THE ROCKS AND TURNED TO STONE.

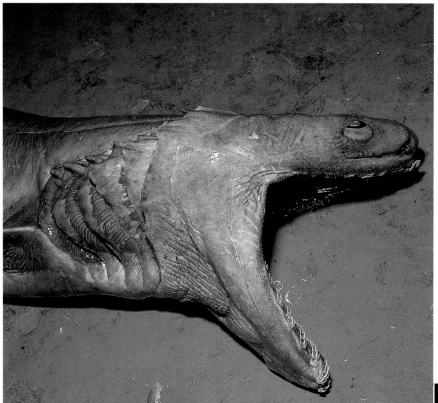

Fossilization is a very rare, chance process. It usually happens only to hard parts, like animal shells, bones, teeth, or horns. Sharks have no shells or bones. Their skeletons are cartilage (see page 39). Much of the information available about their ancient history and ancestors comes from their preserved teeth.

clues to the past

Fossilized sharks' teeth are very common. In life, they were made of enamel and dentine, two of the hardest substances in the animal kingdom. For centuries, people have used them as traditional charms and decorations. Sometimes they were believed to be the teeth of dragons or other monsters. Neils Stenson recognized their true origins (see page 11). Luckily for us, the teeth from different shark species are fairly

above: **The rare frilled shark is regarded as one of the most primitive shark types (see panel on page 42).**

right: **A fossilized tooth, compared to the jaws and teeth of a present-day specimen, show the size of prehistoric sharks.**

S H A R K   S U C C E S S

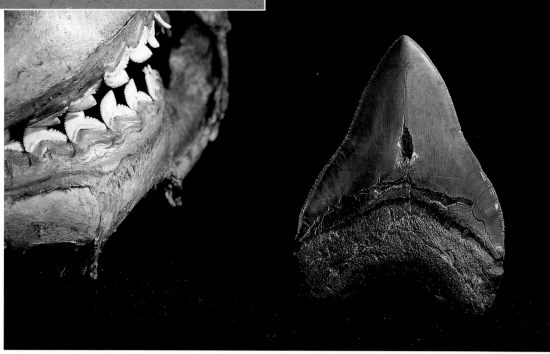

distinctive in size, shape, and make-up. So they can be used to study evolutionary relationships, both today and in the past.

Fossils of shark skeletons are much rarer. In life, the skeleton is made of a relatively soft, light, gristly material called cartilage. This quickly rots after death. The few skeletons that have been preserved, by exceptional circumstances, offer fascinating details about these ancient species.

Skin, muscles, guts, and other soft tissues are preserved even more rarely. However, they do exist. A few precious specimens give impressions of the insides of prehistoric sharks. They are found in very fine-grained sediments, such as the Late Devonian shale rocks along the shores of Lake Erie (see *Cladoselache*, page 36).

a window on the past

Some species have remained almost unchanged from their prehistoric ancestors. These "living fossils" give paleontologists a window on the prehistoric world. For sharks, the elfin or goblin shark is a good example. It was first described for science from its fossilized teeth, 100 million years old. Then the real, living version was discovered in 1898, near Japan, where it had damaged a submarine telegraph cable. The frilled shark and horned shark are also considered to be "living fossils" (see pages 42 and 50).

Sometimes traces of a creature, rather than the actual animal, are preserved. They include footprints, tail drag-marks, and eggshell fragments. For sharks, the main trace fossils are coprolites—preserved excrement or droppings. They can reveal the size and shape of the digestive system. Spiral coprolites show that sharks evolved the spiral valve in their digestive system at an early stage. Some well-preserved coprolites even contain bones and shells of the shark's last supper.

HOW FOSSILS FORM

1. A shark (or other living thing) dies. Its remains sink to the sea bed. The soft flesh and entrails are eaten by scavengers. But the harder parts, like the teeth, and perhaps the skeleton and skin, persist.

2. Mud, sand, and other bits of particles and debris are always sinking and accumulating on the sea bed, as sediments. Gradually the shark's remains become covered.

3. Over hundreds and thousands of years, more sediments collect, and the layers thicken. The deeper ones are squeezed by the weight of those above. Their particles are pressed together and cemented by mineral action.

4. Over millions of years, these massive forces gradually turn the sediments into rocks. The shark's remains change, too. They keep their shape, but they are no longer cartilage or tooth: they are stone.

5. Eventually, continental drift or earthquakes or mountain-building push the fossil-containing rocks to the dry-land surface. Rain, wind, ice, and other forces erode them, exposing the fossils. A passing paleontologist finds them.

ICHTHYOSAUR AND SHARK

SEDIMENTS

FOSSIL BONES

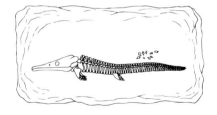

FOSSIL TEETH AND SCALES
(SHARK SKELETON IS NOT BONE)

above: **A shark and an ichthyosaur (an extinct dolphin-shaped reptile) swim above the muddy bottom of a shallow prehistoric sea. After death, the softest, fleshy parts of both slowly rot away. The ichthyosaur's bones and the shark's teeth are all that remain in the fossil record.**

Shark Beginnings

FOSSILS SHOW THAT SHARKS OF VARIOUS KINDS HAVE BEEN AROUND FOR SOME **350** MILLION YEARS. HUMANS CAN BOAST ONLY **1–2** MILLION YEARS.

We have a long way to go, to match the sharks' formidable success.

The fossil record from about 2,000 years to 600 million years ago is tremendously scant and patchy. It shows life forms slowly evolving in the sea, from microscopic single cells, into simple, soft-bodied, jelly-like animals and floppy plant-like organisms.

jelly to shells

above: **A wonderfully preserved shark's tooth** from **the species** *Corehorodon megalodon,* **from the Pliocene epoch, some five million years ago.**

Around 550 million years ago there was a major development—the appearance of hard materials for animal bodies. These could be shaped by natural selection into body casings, weapons for attack, and armor for defense. Over a few tens of millions of years, there was an explosion in evolution, with many different designs of shelled creatures. Molluscs had one or more wraparound shells and tough teeth. Trilobites had furrowed body casings, legs, and claws.

With so many new and predatory animals evolving so quickly, a successful means of escape was vital. There was also food to find, mates to locate, and many other tasks for survival of individual or species, which could be improved by fast movement. Certain creatures evolved a rigid rod of tissue along the inside of the body, like a central supporting column. Bands of muscles on either side of the rod made it bend and flex, from one side to the other, to create a forward movement. The rod is called a notochord, and the creatures with it were the first chordates (see page 48). They swam with a wriggling motion.

A small, transparent, leaflike animal, the lancelet or amphioxus, still survives today, to show us this stage of evolution. It has no proper backbone, fins, jaws, or eyes. It lives half buried in the gravelly bottom of shallow tropical seas,

filtering tiny particles of food from the water. Yet its body has the rudimentary design that was to give rise to all fish, amphibians, reptiles, birds, and mammals.

more design improvements

Evolution continued. The notochord became surrounded by a linked chain of units, the vertebrae (backbones), for extra strength and mobility. Flaplike extensions of the body enlarged, to help give more propulsion and better control. These became the tail and fins.

The pairs of arch-shaped, blood-rich, feathery gills on the sides of the head became more sophisticated, for better breathing underwater. The head itself became the controlling focus of the nerve system, with sensory parts such as eyes and taste buds, and a lump of interwoven nerve fibers, the brain.

The first fish had evolved. They were the earliest members of the great subgroup of chordate animals, known as vertebrates. This was around 400 million years ago, during the geological time called the Devonian Period. Again, a few "living fossils" survive today, to help us understand this stage of evolution. They are the lampreys and hagfish, with rounded, sucker-like mouths. However, these ancient fish lacked one more feature that was to appear, on the evolutionary line to sharks—jaws.

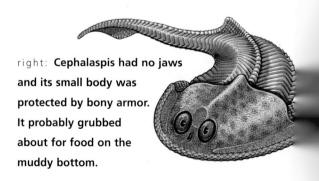

right: **Cephalaspis had no jaws and its small body was protected by bony armor. It probably grubbed about for food on the muddy bottom.**

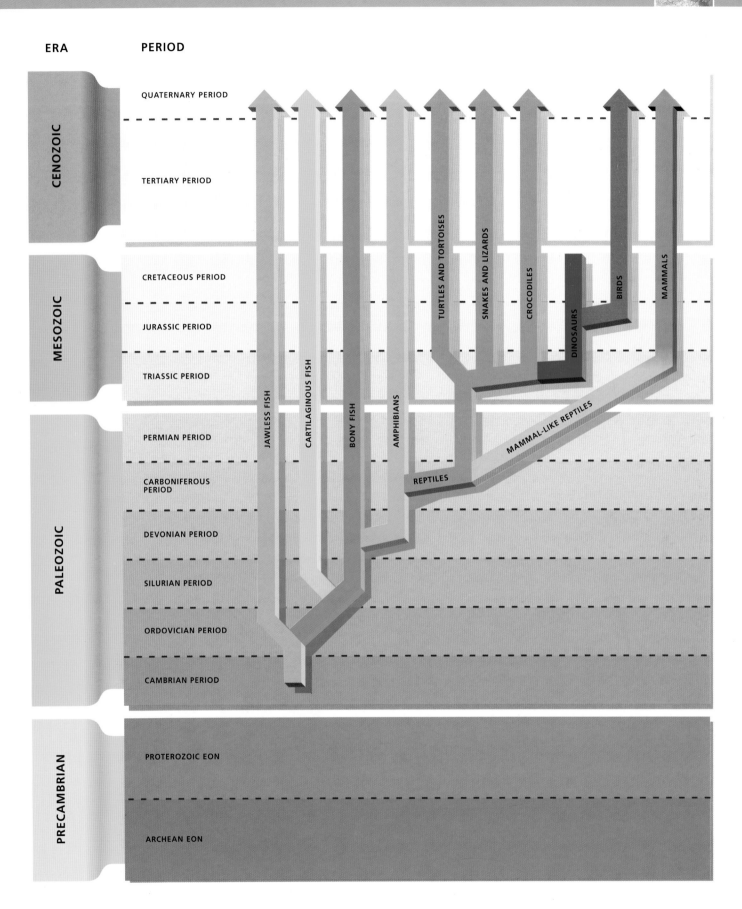

ERA

PERIOD

QUATERNARY PERIOD

TERTIARY PERIOD

CENOZOIC

CRETACEOUS PERIOD

JURASSIC PERIOD

TRIASSIC PERIOD

MESOZOIC

PERMIAN PERIOD

CARBONIFEROUS PERIOD

DEVONIAN PERIOD

SILURIAN PERIOD

ORDOVICIAN PERIOD

CAMBRIAN PERIOD

PALEOZOIC

PROTEROZOIC EON

ARCHEAN EON

PRECAMBRIAN

JAWLESS FISH
CARTILAGINOUS FISH
BONY FISH
AMPHIBIANS
REPTILES
TURTLES AND TORTOISES
SNAKES AND LIZARDS
CROCODILES
DINOSAURS
BIRDS
MAMMALS
MAMMAL-LIKE REPTILES

above: The evolutionary tree of the vertebrates. The ancestors of the vertebrates, the Chordates, lived among the invertebrate animals of the Cambrian. Cartilaginous fish evolved from the main vertebrate branch more than 400 million years ago.

The Age of Sharks

Through evolution, these moved forward, enlarged, and became hinged jaws that could grab, snap, and slice. The appearance of biting jaws opened up a whole new range of feeding possibilities, including predation.

The first fish with jaws were Acanthodians, sometimes called "spiny sharks." They were not true sharks (which had not evolved yet), or even the ancestors of true sharks. But they had a sharklike body shape. Their fins were strengthened with spines along the front edges, for better swimming control. Their jaws were lined with sharp teeth, and they doubtless feasted on their jawless cousins.

end of an era

Alongside the spiny sharks, another branch of the fish evolutionary tree was developing. Many of these had plates of bony armor embedded in their skin, and jaws with sharp, bladelike edges rather than teeth. Some grew to almost 30 feet long, by far the largest animals of their time. The Placoderms reigned supreme in seas, rivers, and lakes, for about 40 million years.

About 360 million years ago, the Devonian Period gave way to the Carboniferous Period. Fossils and rocks show that there were major ecological changes, perhaps in climate and sea levels. The Placoderms faded into extinction. They were replaced by another fish group, the Chondrichthyes, which had already been around for some 40 millions years.

dominating the seas

The Chondrichthyes included the true sharks and their relatives: the skates, rays, and chimaeras. They had skeletons of cartilage, not bone. Their skin was covered with tiny toothlike denticles, not bony plates or scales. Their jaws were lined with rows of teeth which were always developing and being replaced, conveyor-belt fashion, and so were always razor-sharp. Through the Carboniferous Period, they dominated the seas, lakes, and rivers.

One of the best-known early sharks is *Cladoselache*, from 350 million years ago. Its remains were beautifully preserved in the Black Cleveland Shales of Lake Erie, and were found in the 1880s by the fossil-hunter Dr William Kepler. The fine-grained sedimentary rocks contain traces of skeleton, skin, and even muscles.

Cladoselache had a slim body about five feet long, with two pairs of ventral (underside) fins and two spined dorsal (topside) fins. The rear of the body narrowed and bent upward, with a large caudal or tail fin on the underside. This design, the heterocercal tail, is found in all modern sharks. It had large eyes, a short snout, and many teeth, indicating an open-ocean predator that hunted by sight.

THE FRILLED SHARK— A "LIVING FOSSIL"

The frilled shark is very like *Cladoselache*, although nearer seven feet long. Its mouth is at the front of its head, with nostrils on top. (Modern sharks have their mouths and nostrils on the head's underside.) Its teeth are also primitive in shape, arranged in 20 rows with five teeth in each. This shark can protrude and gape its jaws widely, to engulf its deep-water prey of octopus and squid. The frilled shark also still has a rod of cartilage, the notocord, running along the center of its body from skull to tail. Its lateral line system for sensing vibrations and movements in the water (see page 100) is an open groove, rather than being in a part-buried tube in the skin, as other sharks.

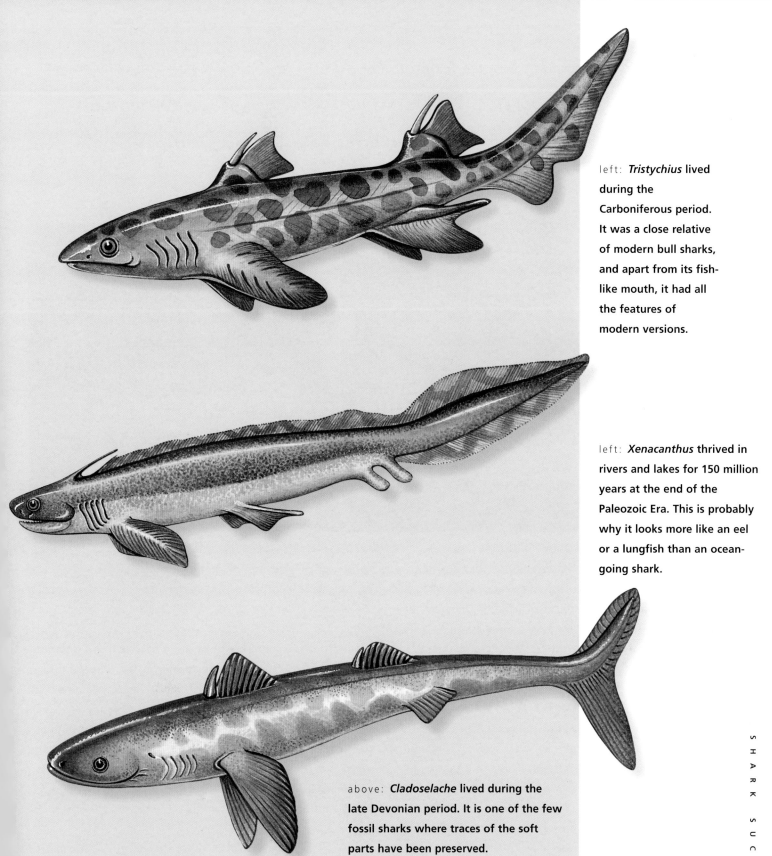

left: *Tristychius* lived during the Carboniferous period. It was a close relative of modern bull sharks, and apart from its fish-like mouth, it had all the features of modern versions.

left: *Xenacanthus* thrived in rivers and lakes for 150 million years at the end of the Paleozoic Era. This is probably why it looks more like an eel or a lungfish than an ocean-going shark.

above: *Cladoselache* lived during the late Devonian period. It is one of the few fossil sharks where traces of the soft parts have been preserved.

Shark Kith and Kin

AS EVOLUTION CONTINUED, THE MAIN GROUPS OF FISH AS WE KNOW THEM TODAY BECAME ESTABLISHED. THE MAIN DIVISION IS BETWEEN THE JAWLESS FISH OR AGNATHANS, THE CARTILAGINOUS FISH OR CHONDRICHTHYES, AND THE BONY FISH, OSTEICHTHYES.

above: **Amphioxus, the lancelet, is a fish-like creature that has a notocord, the forerunner of a true backbone. It is a chordate, but not a vertebrate (see page 40).**

above right: **While sharks ruled the seas, other types of fish developed limbs and became amphibians. The salamander is a modern amphibian.**

The Chrondrichthyes are split into two groups: the sharks, skates, and rays form Elasmobranchs; and the ratfish or chimaeras are the Holocephalians. The Elasmobranchs are divided again in two: the skates and rays (Batoidea) and the sharks themselves (Selachii).

bony fish

Today, the bony fish (Osteichthyes) are masters of the watery world. There are some 400 species of sharks, within a total of about 700 species of cartilaginous fish. But there are well over 23,000 species of bony fish already discovered and described, and doubtless more waiting to be recognized.

Bony fish, as their name implies, have skeletons made of bone. Most also have a bony plate or operculum as a gill cover, and overlapping, bone-based scales. The most ancient groups are coelacanths, lungfish, sturgeons, bowfins, and paddlefish. There are hundreds of other familiar types, such as salmon, pike, tuna, catfish, goldfish, and sticklebacks. They have successfully colonized every watery habitat, fresh and salty, from marsh and swamp to the darkest, coldest ocean depths. Eels can wriggle over land, and mudskippers and climbing perches can even ascend trees. It's thought that amphibians evolved from certain bony fishes, resembling lungfish or coelacanths, around 350–400 million years ago.

ratfish

There are about 23 species of ratfish, also known as chimaeras, or rabbitfish. *Chimaera* is derived from the name of a Greek monster that had a goat's body, lion's head, and serpent's tail—reflecting the mixed-up features of the ratfish.

These include a disproportionately big head, forward-pointing "beak" formed from large rabbit-like fused front teeth, poisonous dorsal spine, and long, stringy, ratlike tail.

Ratfish have many other mixed features. They have only four gill openings or slits, fewer than a shark. But, as with bony fish, the gills are protected by a platelike gill cover or operculum. Water is drawn in through the nostrils, rather than through the mouth, as in sharks. The spinal column consists of separate rings of cartilage around a notochord. Young ratfish have skin denticles, like sharks, but most are lost by the time they reach adulthood.

Ratfish swim awkwardly, by flapping their pectoral fins in the manner of a ray. They spend most of their time resting on the deep sea bed, propped up on their fintips. Here they feed on bottom-living shellfish, which they crunch up with the strong beak. The ratfish snout is covered with sense organs that can detect electrical currents and waterborne scents, and the eyes are huge—all adaptations to finding their way and prey in the inky blackness.

above: **Sea-squirts, or ascidians, are simple seashore creatures. Their tadpole-like young forms, larvae, have the merest beginnings of a backbone-like structure, suggesting how the whole vertebrate group could have evolved.**

below: **Ratfish form one of the two main groups of cartilaginous fish, the other being sharks, skates, and rays.**

THE THREE GROUPS OF CARTILAGINOUS FISH HAVE DIFFERENT MAIN PREFERENCES. WHILE SHARKS ARE FOUND IN ALL THE OCEANS, AT ALL TEMPERATURES AND DEPTHS, MANY SPECIES LIVE IN THE OPEN WATERS OF THE TROPICS AND SUBTROPICS.

Ratfish dwell in cold, deep seas. Skates and rays are chiefly creatures of the sea bed.

There are over 300 species in the skate and ray group, including the guitarfish and sawfish. They are all adapted for bottom living and feed on other animals there, such as flatfish, clams and other shellfish, shrimps and other crustaceans, worms, and carrion. The "wings" on the side of the body are enlarged pectoral fins. As the ray undulates or ripples them, it moves through the water. The eyes are on the top of the head, and water is pumped in through the holes or spiracles near them, over the gills, and out through the gill slits on the underside. Thus a ray can rest on the muddy bottom, breathe easily (many sharks must keep swimming in order to breathe), and keep watch for danger and prey.

electric action

Skates and rays, like sharks (see page 102), are sensitive to the electric field which travels through the water from active animal muscles. (We detect these same types of pulses from our own muscle as an electrocardiogram, ECG.) This electrical sense helps them to navigate in dark or cloudy water, and locate prey in the sand (see page 102).

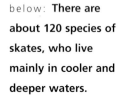

below: **There are about 120 species of skates, who live mainly in cooler and deeper waters.**

Electric rays go a stage further. Blocks of branchial muscles on either side of the front body have evolved to produce huge bursts of electricity, 300 volts or more. The ray embraces its prey in its wings, shocks it to stunned inaction, then grinds up its body using its flat, slablike teeth.

Stingrays have a venomous serrated spine partway along the whiplike tail. The poison is mainly for defense, as the ray lies buried in the sand, waiting for prey. The Atlantic stingray is roughly the size of a dinner plate. The smooth stingray is ten times bigger and has a spine a foot long. Two other stingray species from South America live in rivers. They are the only cartilaginous fish completely adapted to fresh water.

The biggest ray is the huge manta or devilfish, with a "wingspan" of more than 19 feet. It can leap from the water, flopping back with a gigantic splash. Like the biggest shark, the whale shark, the manta filter-feeds on small animals and plants in the plankton.

guitars and swords

The sawfish's snout is like a chainsaw, flat and long, and edged with pointed teeth. It is used to dig food out of mud, to slash at swimming prey, and for defense. Apart from the snout, this cartilaginous fish resembles a shark in overall appearance.

Guitarfish, shaped as their name suggests, are sometimes called shark-rays and prefer sandy shallows. They also feed on bottom-living shellfish and other creatures, which are crushed with flattened teeth. The giant guitarfish of the Indian and Pacific Oceans grows to 10 feet in length, and looks like a combination of large shark and saw-less sawfish.

above: **A sawfish marooned on the beach of Barrow Island, Western Australia.**

left: **The guitarfish resembles a shark-ray hybrid, but is a true member of the skate-and-ray group.**

right: **Small fish trail the largest ray, a huge Pacific manta.**

Classifying Sharks

THE STUDY OF THE LIVING WORLD INVOLVES SORTING LIFE FORMS INTO GROUPS WITH SIMILAR

CHARACTERISTICS AND CLOSE EVOLUTIONARY RELATIONSHIPS.

The science of taxonomy, or classification, underlies all of biology. It is a level-by-level system, or hierarchy. The main groups are kingdoms, which are divided into subgroups called phyla (singular: phylum), which are, in turn, divided into classes, then orders, families, genera (singular: genus), and finally the basic taxonomic "unit:": the species.

The true sharks, Selachii, are a relatively well-studied animal group. But their taxonomy is by no means precisely defined. Even the number of species varies, from under 400 to well over 450, according to the classification schemes of different experts.

kingdom and phylum

In the overall classification scheme used by most scientists today, there are five major groups, the kingdoms. Sharks, of course, are in the kingdom Animalia, along with well over one million other species, from gnats to ourselves.

At the next level down, sharks belong to the phylum Chordata—the chordates, animals that possess a notochord (see page 40) or a backbone derived from it. This phylum is then split at a halfway level into two sub-phyla. The sharks' subphylum is Vertebrata, the vertebrates, taking in animals with a vertebral column. This includes all fish, amphibians, reptiles, birds and mammals.

class and order

There are about ten classes of vertebrates. Four are amphibians, reptiles, birds, and mammals. The rest are types of fish. Sharks are in the class Chondrichthyes, cartilaginous fish. Another class is Osteichthyes, bony fish. This scheme has replaced the older one whereby all fish were lumped together into one class, Pisces. The new system reflects better the diverse evolutionary origins of these main fish groups.

Class Chondrichthyes is split into two sub-classes, as we saw on page 44. These are

above: **A dwarf shark rests 3,280 feet below the surface of the Atlantic Ocean. It is usually classified in the shark order Scymnorhinidae.**

opposite right:
The largest shark, the whale shark, has the family Rhincodontidae all to itself.

Elasmobranchs, which include sharks, skates and rays, and Holocephali, ratfish or chimaeras.

Elasmobranchs are in turn grouped into two main super-orders: Batoidea, skates and rays, and Selachii, true sharks. The Selachii (or Selachimorpha) are divided into about 12 main orders, as you can see on pages 50–53.

a question of judgment

The above scheme is not universally accepted. Some experts contend that true sharks form a whole class, not a sub-class or a super-order. And when all the extinct groups from prehistory are added in, it becomes many times more complex. Variations in the scheme arise when experts disagree about which features of an animal are most significant. They may be aspects of its physical body, which is anatomy; or its internal functioning and chemistry, which is physiology; or, increasingly, its genetic make-up.

The general trend is that, as the levels become lower and the groups smaller, the creatures in them are more similar and more closely related.

A CLASSIFICATION OF LIVING SHARKS

Kingdom	Animals
Sub-kingdom	Metazoans (many-celled)
Phylum	Chordates (possessing a notochord)
Sub-phylum	Vertebrates (possessing a backbone)
Super-class	Gnathostomata (jawed vertebrates)
Class	Chondrichthyes (cartilaginous skeletons)
Sub-class	Elasmobranchs (ribbon-like gills)
Super-order	Selachimorphs (shark-shaped)

NAMING NAMES

Every type of living thing described by scientists is given an internationally accepted two-part name, known as its binomial nomenclature. The first part is the genus, the second is the individual species. The tongue-twisting words are often derived from Latin or Ancient Greek, and describe some aspect of the organism. We are *Homo sapiens*, "Wise human." The megamouth shark is *Megachasma pelagios*, "Huge hole of the sea."

right: **The Pacific angelshark belongs to the order known as Squatiniformes, and shows some similarities with rays.**

TRUE LIVING SHARKS (NOT NECESSARILY FOSSIL ONES) SHARE MANY FEATURES. THESE INCLUDE A CARTILAGINOUS SKELETON, FAIRLY INFLEXIBLE FINS, TINY TOOTHLIKE SKIN DENTICLES, AND LACK OF GILL COVERS.

above: **The moses shark of the Red Sea belongs to the genus Mustelus, which includes various smooth-hounds and dogfish, in the Triakidae family.**

opposite right: **Port Jackson sharks tend to come together and rest in groups during the mating season, as seen here in Jervis Bay, New South Wales, Australia.**

Sharks also have individual features which help with their further classification into several major groups as follows.

• frills and gills

The most primitive or ancient group, or order, of living sharks is the Hexanchiformes. It includes two families. One, Chlamydoselachidae, has just one "living" species, the frilled shark, *Chlamydoselachus anguineus*. It is named from the frill-like covers to its six pairs of gill slits. This shark has a notochord as the main stiffening in its back, and only one dorsal fin. Its jaws and teeth resemble fossil species from 350 million years ago (see page 42).

The second family is the Hexanchidae, the comb-toothed sharks, cow sharks, or six- and seven-gilled sharks (most other sharks have only five pairs of gill slits). The five species live in deep water, have only one dorsal fin, and their jaws and vertebrae resemble their fossil counterparts from 190 million years ago. The name comes from the comblike teeth on the lower jaw.

• bulls and horns

Another very ancient order is the Heterodontiformes—"different teeth." They are known as bullhead sharks and lived in the seas 220 million years ago, when the first dinosaurs appeared on land. Today they include the six or so species of horn or Port Jackson sharks.

• spines and lanterns

Spiny-finned sharks belong to the order Squaliformes, more usually known as the dogfish sharks. There are about 70 species divided between several families. The Squalidae includes the spined shark, spiny dogfish (also known as the spurdog), dogfish shark, sleeper shark, and lantern shark. The Scymnorhinidae comprise the spineless dogfish and dwarf sharks. The Echinorhinidae are the bramble sharks, named for their knobbly skin. The Oxynotidae are the rough sharks.

• saws

The order Pristiophoriformes contains five species of sawsharks. They are flattened for bottom-dwelling, more like skates and rays than sharks. Indeed, the elongated, flat snout edged with sharp teeth is very similar to the "saw" of a sawfish. But sawfish and sawsharks are only distant cousins. The sawshark's saw-teeth vary in size, while sawfish's are all the same length.

• angels and monks

The Squatiniformes order takes in about ten species of angelsharks, sometimes called monkfish. They are also flattened and lie on the bottom, waiting to ambush prey. They have several raylike features and may represent an evolutionary link between sharks and rays.

THE TWO LARGEST ORDERS OF "TYPICAL" SHARKS ARE THE MACKEREL AND REQUIEM SHARKS.

THEY ARE MOSTLY SLEEK, FAST-SWIMMING PREDATORS WITH ROWS OF POINTED TEETH, TWO

DORSAL FINS, A SINGLE FIN, AND FIVE PAIRS OF GILL SLITS.

above: **The basking shark, a member of the order Lamniformes, the mackerel sharks, shows its vast gape as it feeds.**

• mackerels

The order Lamniformes has some 15 species in seven families. Known generally as mackerel sharks, many are famous or infamous in their own right. They include the basking shark (Cetorhinidae), and the great white, mako and other "typical" mackerel sharks (Lamnidae), mostly large and powerful beasts of the wide open water, with few enemies and fewer friends. Other groups are the threshers (Alopiidae), crocodile sharks (Pseudocarchariidae), goblin sharks (Mitsukurinidae) with their strange unicorn-like pointed foreheads, and sand tigers,

gray nurse or raggedtooth (Odontaspididae). The curious, recently discovered megamouth shark has its own family, Megachasmidae.

• ground sharks

The 100 or so species of ground sharks in the order Carcharhiniformes are the most "shark-like" of all sharks. Most are streamlined hunters of open water, often swimming with the dorsal fin above the surface. The main family, Carcharinidae, is also known as requiem sharks and includes tiger sharks, white-tips, black-tips, and blue sharks. Other families are the

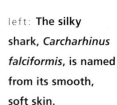

left: **The silky shark, *Carcharhinus falciformis*, is named from its smooth, soft skin.**

below: **Epaulette sharks, *Hemiscyllium ocellotum*, are among the few spotty sharks.**

hammerheads and bonnet sharks (Sphyrnidae), hound sharks such as the tope, smooth dogfish, the soupfin or oil shark of culinary fame and the beautifully-patterned leopard shark (Triakidae), barbeled hound sharks (Leptochariidae), weasel sharks (Hemigaleidae), catsharks, also the nursehound and swell shark, and perhaps the most familiar shark of all to Europeans, the lesser spotted dogfish (Scyliorhinidae), finback cat sharks (Proscylliidae), and false cat sharks (Pseudotriakidae).

• carpets and nurses

The last main order of sharks is the Orectolobiformes, with about 30 species in seven families. Among them are carpet sharks and wobbegongs, epaulette sharks and nurse sharks, blind and zebra sharks. They tend to lie or swim slowly on the sea bed. One family, Rhincodontidae, within this order contains one species—the largest shark and biggest fish of all, the whale shark *Rhincodon typus*.

right: **Gray reef shark, another member of the genus Carcharhinus.**

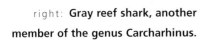

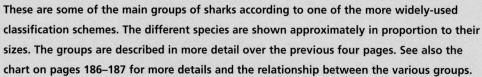

These are some of the main groups of sharks according to one of the more widely-used classification schemes. The different species are shown approximately in proportion to their sizes. The groups are described in more detail over the previous four pages. See also the chart on pages 186–187 for more details and the relationship between the various groups.

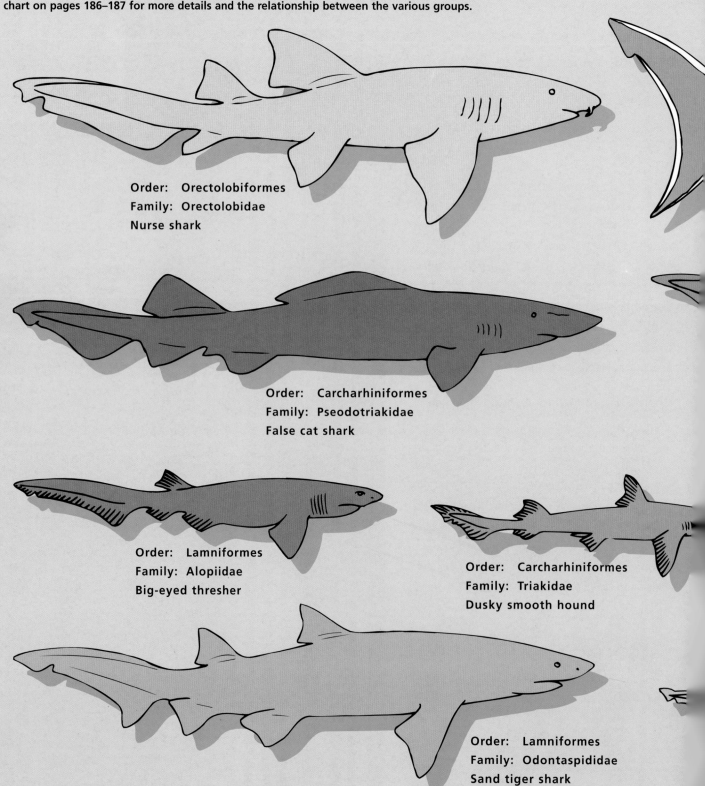

Order: Orectolobiformes
Family: Orectolobidae
Nurse shark

Order: Carcharhiniformes
Family: Pseodotriakidae
False cat shark

Order: Lamniformes
Family: Alopiidae
Big-eyed thresher

Order: Carcharhiniformes
Family: Triakidae
Dusky smooth hound

Order: Lamniformes
Family: Odontaspididae
Sand tiger shark

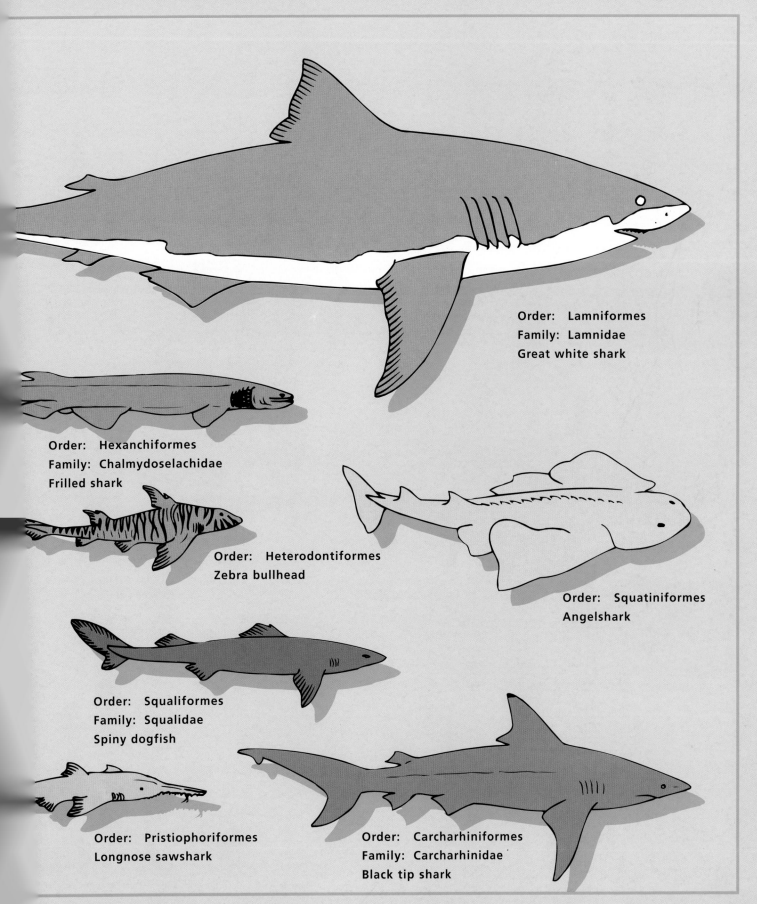

Order: Lamniformes
Family: Lamnidae
Great white shark

Order: Hexanchiformes
Family: Chalmydoselachidae
Frilled shark

Order: Heterodontiformes
Zebra bullhead

Order: Squatiniformes
Angelshark

Order: Squaliformes
Family: Squalidae
Spiny dogfish

Order: Pristiophoriformes
Longnose sawshark

Order: Carcharhiniformes
Family: Carcharhinidae
Black tip shark

CHAPTER 3

Ecology and Biology

SHARKS ARE AN INTEGRAL PART OF THE BIGGEST NATURAL SYSTEM ON THE PLANET—THE MARINE ECOSYSTEM.

above: **A whitetip reef shark swims among fellow fish, which are largely unconcerned by its massive presence.**

above right: **The flattened shape of certain sharks and rays, like the shovel-nosed ray, immediately suggests a bottom-dweller.**

previous page: **Shallow water, large torpedo shape, fin cutting the surface, add up to a worrying scenario. But most large sharks rarely venture into such minimal depth.**

To understand how sharks have evolved and diversified to exploit almost every type of food, in almost every part of every sea and ocean, it helps to know something about the background to this ecosystem.

The marine environment is the largest and oldest of all Earth's habitats. Salt water covers more than two-thirds of the world's surface. Its average depth is about 1¾ miles, but it ranges from almost nothing along shallow shores, to a few hundred yards across the continental shelves, to more than six miles in the deepest abyssal trenches.

on the sea bed

On land, we are used to many different conditions and habitats—mountains, valleys, woods, grassland, hot desert, steamy rainforest, icy tundra. Likewise, the ocean is far from uniform. It is divided into many different kinds of habitats, each with vastly different characteristics.

The sea bed is the benthic habitat—that is, the habitat of benthos, the flora and fauna that live at the bottom of seas and lakes. Its topography varies enormously, from flat plains to gentle hills and valleys, towering seamounts, sheet cliffs and plunging submarine canyons. Sea-bed material also varies, from bare rock to pebbles and gravels, sparkling sand, and thick, gooey mud. The ocean floor is subjected to a constant "rain" of material from above, such as dead bodies, animal wastes, and bits of detritus. Worms, shellfish, flatfish, and similar benthic creatures live there. If the sea is shallow and light can penetrate, algal plants (seaweeds) also thrive.

the open waters

Above the benthic layer is the pelagic habitat—or open water. This can be divided in two ways. One is by latitude, from equator to pole, as shown on page 64. The second is vertically, into three main layers of depth, depending on the degree of penetration by sunlight. In turn, this depends mainly on the cloudiness or turbidity of the water.

The uppermost layer, to an average depth of 330 feet, is relatively bright and sunlit. Algae thrive here, and are the basic food for all ocean creatures, as shown on page 60. This surface water is also under the influence of global weather patterns and its temperatures fluctuate greatly. Most of the well-known sharks live in this uppermost layer.

twilight to blackness

The middle layer ranges from about 330 to 3,300 feet. It is a twilight zone, too dark for most plants to grow, and occupied mainly by fish and other creatures with huge eyes, who hunt each other in the gloom.

Below about 3,300 feet, it is pitch-black. The pressure of the waters above is gigantic. Temperatures and any water movements, or currents, are relatively constant. It is a world we have hardly explored. Yet it is the biggest subhabitat of the marine environment. Many animal species almost certainly wait to be discovered here, including more sharks.

MONSTER FROM THE DEEP

In 1976 a United States Navy ship was trailing its parachute anchor 450 feet deep, near Hawaii. When the line was winched in, a huge shark was entangled within it. The species was completely new to science. It was nearly 15 feet long, weighed 1,650 pounds, and had a colossal scooplike mouth with 1,000 tiny teeth on the lower jaw. It was nicknamed "megamouth," and later, after intensive study, given the scientific name *Megachasma pelagios*. In the following 20 years, about seven more "megamouths" were landed for study. They are weak-swimming tropical sharks that filter tiny organisms from the water. There is speculation whether their "lips" glow in the dark. The latest thinking is that tissue in the mouth reflects light from the luminous organisms it eats.

right: **The megamouth shark is a fairly recent discovery, from the 1970s. Its existence indicates that there may well be other deep-sea sharks which are as yet unknown to science.**

left: **The blue shark's prominent countershading shows a near-surface inhabitant.**

Food Webs and Chains

LIVING THINGS DEPEND ON EACH OTHER FOR NOURISHMENT, IN COMPLEX AND INTERLINKED

PATTERNS OF FOOD CHAINS, FOOD WEBS, NUTRIENT CYCLES, AND POPULATION PYRAMIDS.

above: **Aggressive and dangerous, a Galapagos shark feeding on mackerel.**

Many sharks may be fierce predators, but they depend ultimately, like all life, on the sun.

The basic food in any habitat is plants or plant-like organisms that trap the sun's light energy; they do this by the process of photosynthesis. On land, they are familiar as flowers, grasses, and trees. In the open ocean, they are much less obvious. They are drifting, microscopic, single-celled algal organisms, called phytoplankton. There are two main kinds, diatoms thrive in cooler waters, while silicoflagellates live in warm waters. At the coasts around the oceans, and in shallow waters, much larger algae, which are true plants, grow. They are seaweeds such as wracks, oarweeds, dulse, carragheen, and sea lettuce.

herbivores

Animals that eat only plants or plant-like organisms are called herbivores. Near the seashore, they include molluscs such as limpets and winkles, grazing on seaweeds. In the open ocean, they are mainly zooplankton—tiny animals and animal-like organisms that eat the phytoplankton. Some are just-hatched, miniature developing larvae (immature stages) of larger creatures such as crabs, shellfish, worms, jellyfish, starfish, squid, and fish called meroplankton. Others, the holoplankton such as arrow-worms, spend all their lives as small drifters.

carnivores

Animals that eat other animals are called carnivores. In the sea, the tiny animals of the zooplankton are eaten by their larger cousins, such as small fish and shrimps. These, in turn, are eaten by bigger fish, squid, and other predators. And so the food chains build up, and in general, the carnivores get bigger.

Most sharks are carnivorous. They come at or near the ends of their food chains, so they are known as top carnivores or top predators. Their hunting not only feeds themselves, but helps to keep their prey, such as fish, seals or squid, in peak condition by weeding out the old, diseased, and poorly adapted individuals. Sharks are a potent force in ensuring the survival of the fittest, and thereby driving the process of evolution.

detritivores

Nature wastes nothing and recycles everything. The dead and dying bodies of animals and plants, carrion, animal excrement, and any other nutritious bits and pieces are eaten by detritus-feeders or detritivores.

They include shellfish such as mussels and crustaceans like crabs. Some sharks are notorious carrion-eaters, playing a significant part in ridding the ocean of rotting carcasses.

FILTER-FEEDERS

The distinctions between, for example, herbivores and carnivores, are far from complete. The same animal, such as a Port Jackson shark, may eat plant matter, animal flesh, and carrion. This is how food chains become interwoven into food webs.

The vast floating "slicks" of plankton are a complex mixture of tiny plants and animals. They are consumed by oceanic filter-feeders, including sharks and great whales. Oddly, these tiny food items supply some of the biggest shark species—the whale shark, basking shark, and megamouth.

above: **Bigger fish are eaten by even bigger fish, as a huge tiger shark feeds on a smaller individual from the same species. The tigers hunt mainly just below the surface.**

61

Shark Sizes and Numbers

THE LARGEST SHARK, AND THE BIGGEST FISH OF ALL, IS THE WHALE SHARK. THIS FILTER-FEEDER IS CLAIMED TO REACH **66** FEET IN LENGTH AND **44** TONS IN WEIGHT.

above: **Gray sharks gather at a Pacific reef, seeming common here— but relatively rare in the overall scheme of ecology.**

Authenticated records stand at 12.6 metres (41 feet) and 21 tonnes (23 tons) for a measured whale shark, and about 17 metres (55½ feet) and 30 tonnes (33 tons) for a relatively accurate, close-to estimation of another specimen.

The second biggest is another filter-feeder and more common, the basking shark. Reliable measurements include one specimen 12.3 metres (just over 40 feet) long, weighing 16 tonnes (17½ tons). About 32 feet and 5–6 tons is a good average.

largest and smallest

The largest predatory shark, and the biggest of all hunting fish, is the legendary great white— also called the man-eater, white pointer, or white-death shark. This is the "star" of many ocean horror stories. Great whites usually grow to about 16 feet 6 inches in length and 1,100 pounds in weight. The largest reliably measured specimen was 6.4 metres (21 feet) and, being an

obese female, weighed an amazing 3.3 tonnes (3½ tons). Another giant landed in the Azores was perhaps 30 feet long. Stories abound of even larger great whites that "got away." Some were claimed to reach 40 feet in length.

The next-biggest hunting sharks are probably the tiger, Greenland, and six-gilled sharks, which may exceed 20 feet long.

The great white would be beaten by its now extinct cousin, the great-toothed shark or *Megalodon*. This giant died out perhaps 12,000 years ago. Only its fossilized teeth remain, but reconstructions from these indicate a body length of up to 50 feet.

The smallest shark, at just six inches in length, is the aptly-named dwarf or midwater lantern shark, *Squaliolus laticaudus*. It lives in the West Pacific Ocean. A common and more familiar small shark is the lesser spotted dogfish, at just over three feet long.

shark numbers

The great white shark, despite its fame and image, is a rare fish. The total world population may number fewer than 10,000. Indeed, most sharks are relatively uncommon. Their low numbers reflect their role as big predators. Top carnivores must always be less numerous than their prey, or they would run out of food.

The megamouth and frilled shark are rarely seen so it is not known how many of them exist. Only a handful of specimens have ever been studied. Whale sharks are also rarely sighted, although their habit of cruising just below the surface makes their sightings proportionally more frequent.

In general, smaller sharks are more common. Dogfish abound along many rocky coasts, probably numbering millions. One of the world's more abundant large fish is believed to be the oceanic white-tip shark (*Carcharhinus longimanus*). It thrives throughout the warm waters of the Pacific and Atlantic Oceans.

BIGGER THAN BIG

The only animals in the ocean which are larger than the biggest sharks are the great whales. Of course, they are not fish, but mammals. They breathe air and have warm blood. The largest is the blue whale, which can reach 98 feet in length and 165 tons in weight.

Bony fish are small in comparison to sharks. Heaviest is the plate-shaped ocean sunfish, which reaches almost 10 feet in length and perhaps 2¾ tons in weight. Much longer is the oarfish or ribbonfish, at 23 feet or more. But it is very slim and eel-like, and weighs comparatively little.

above: **Dogfish, like this spotted dogfish, are among the most numerous` sharks. The prefix "dog" meant common and standard, even over-familiar, as in the flowers known as dog roses.**

left: **A dangerous and now endangered species, the great white.**

From Tropics to Poles

SHARKS ARE FOUND THROUGHOUT THE WORLD'S OCEANS. THERE ARE RELATIVELY FEW SPECIES AND INDIVIDUALS IN COLD POLAR SEAS, AND MORE IN TEMPERATE WATERS.

Most species, especially the larger meat-eaters, prefer warm tropical waters. Humans prefer the same, when holidaying. This is reflected in shark-attack statistics, with most incidents in water of about 75°F.

warm-water sharks

Most of the sleek predatory sharks thrive in the Tropics, the seas on either side of the Equator, where the water is warmer than 70°F. The oceanic white-tip is probably the most common, in all tropical oceans—Atlantic, Indian, and Pacific. The blue shark is also found in tropical and subtropical seas around the world. The whale shark also prefers warm water, but this is rarely seen.

There are several species of hammerhead sharks, each occupying its own particular region of open ocean. The scalloped hammerhead is found in all tropical waters. The winged hammerhead is found mainly in the subtropical Pacific and Indian Oceans. Their close cousins, the bonnethead sharks, live in the east Pacific and west Atlantic.

temperate sharks

Some sharks frequent temperate waters, at temperatures of about 50–70°F. One is the great white, found off the coasts of North and South America, Europe, South Africa, and the Mediterranean, Eastern and Southeast Asia, and Australasia.

The basking shark is found in a wide variety of waters, from the Tropics almost to the polar

below: **The lemon shark frequents warmer waters of the West Atlantic, from New Jersey, down through the Caribbean to northern Brazil.**

above: **Bonnet-head or shovel-head sharks, about 5 feet long, often enter shallow bays and estuaries.**

seas. Mako sharks live in temperate regions, and some tropical ones. Thresher sharks once had a wide distribution, as far north as Norway. But overfishing has reduced their numbers in cooler seas; although they are still found in the English Channel. Now they occur only in warmer temperate and subtropical areas.

cold-water sharks

Where the water temperature averages less than 50°F, the sharks tend to be less numerous and more sluggish, such as the smooth-hound and spurdog. These regions include the North Atlantic and North Pacific, the Arctic Ocean—plus the great depths of all the oceans, far away from the warming sun. There are no known sharks in the great Southern Ocean around Antarctica.

One of the best-known cold-water sharks is the Greenland, gurry, or sleeper shark, *Somniosus microcephalus*. Big (up to 16½ feet) and lazy, it has been found in waters within the Arctic Circle. It feeds mainly on bottom-living shellfish, but also hunts seals, porpoises, and sea birds at the surface, and even takes carrion.

The porbeagle, another cold-water shark, lives in the Northern Atlantic and has been found as far north as Iceland. Far from sluggish, it is a type of mackerel shark, and it chases herring and mackerel near the surface.

above: **The cookie-cutter, which snips lumps off bigger creatures, is found in tropical and subtropical waters across the Atlantic and Pacific oceans.**

Where Sharks Live

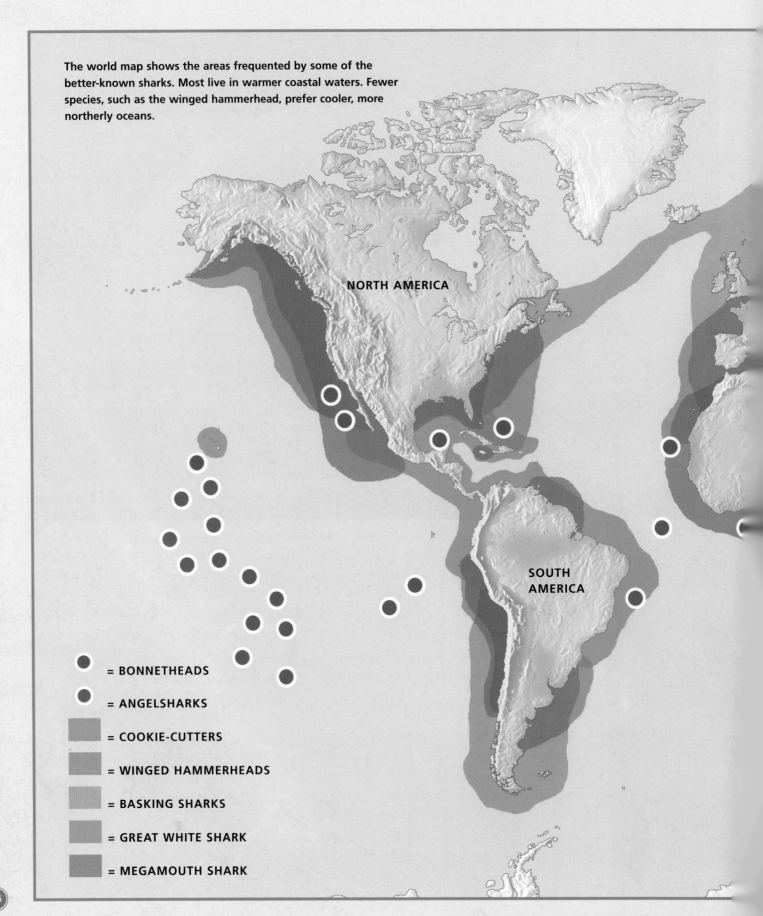

The world map shows the areas frequented by some of the better-known sharks. Most live in warmer coastal waters. Fewer species, such as the winged hammerhead, prefer cooler, more northerly oceans.

NORTH AMERICA

SOUTH AMERICA

= BONNETHEADS

= ANGELSHARKS

= COOKIE-CUTTERS

= WINGED HAMMERHEADS

= BASKING SHARKS

= GREAT WHITE SHARK

= MEGAMOUTH SHARK

ECOLOGY AND BIOLOGY

EUROPE

CHINA

INDIA

AUSTRALIA

SHARKS ARE FOUND AT ALL DEPTHS IN THE SEAS. SOME BASK IN THE WARM SUNLIT WATER OR CHASE PREY JUST BELOW THE SURFACE.

above: **A tawny nurse shark prowls sand and rocks in the shallows of the Australian coast.**

Some sharks seemingly doze at the bottom of the seabed, waiting for food to come to them. A shark's coloration, body shape, and swimming skill indicate its preferred water depth, lifestyle and food source.

shallow-water sharks

The majority of sharks live in warm, shallow waters, down to about 650 feet. Most other sea creatures live here too, and provide the sharks' diet. Spurdogs form huge single-sex shoals just offshore. White-tip reef sharks and nurse sharks laze sluggishly on the bottom by day, but become swift, fierce hunters at night.

Angelsharks, sawsharks, and carpet sharks spend almost all their time on the shallow sea bed. They have unstreamlined bodies and appropriate camouflage—carpet sharks look like weedy, knobbly rocks, while angelsharks resemble the smoothness of the sandy bottom. Swellsharks are also shallow-water fish. They are named from their ability to inhale water or air and enlarge like a balloon, to appear bigger and fiercer, for better defense.

open-ocean sharks

The great predatory groups, the mackerel and requiem sharks, cruise the sunlit upper layers of the open oceans. They can find food by sight as well as scent. Their streamlined bodies are countershaded, dark on the upper surface and lighter on the underside. This provides camouflage when viewed from below or above, and also from the side, since it counteracts the sun's shadowing effect on the belly.

Some species can descend deeper if the need arises. Great whites have been caught below 4,000 feet.

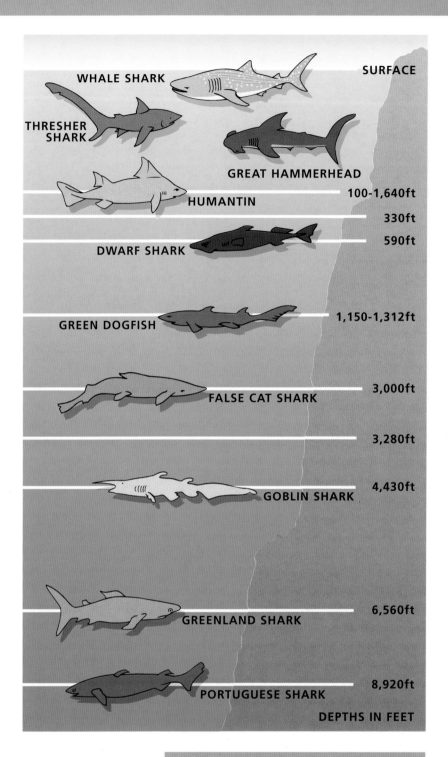

WHALE SHARK

SURFACE

THRESHER
SHARK

GREAT HAMMERHEAD

HUMANTIN

100-1,640ft

330ft

590ft

DWARF SHARK

GREEN DOGFISH

1,150-1,312ft

FALSE CAT SHARK

3,000ft

3,280ft

GOBLIN SHARK

4,430ft

GREENLAND SHARK

6,560ft

PORTUGUESE SHARK

8,920ft

DEPTHS IN FEET

above: **The chart
shows representative
shark species from
different depths.
They frequent these
levels primarily
because that is where
their food lives.
NB Sharks not drawn
to scale**

THE DEEPEST SHARKS

The deepest shark catch was a Portuguese
shark, from 8,776 feet. A strange bug-eyed
shark, species unknown, peered into a
French deep-sea submersible at 12,795 feet.
No doubt there are many more mysterious
sharks in the immense deep-sea habitat.

deeper-water and deep-sea-bed sharks

The diminutive dwarf shark is found mainly in gloomy waters 1,000–3,000 feet deep. Its luminous (light-emitting) organs help it to find food in such deep water. The velvet belly shark, which also has light-producing organs, dwells between 2,300 and 6,550 feet down. *Centrophorus*, a widespread shark with spiny dorsal fins, is found at similar depths in all tropical and temperate seas. Catsharks and false catsharks swim in midwater blackness below 3,300 feet.

The inky blackness of the deep benthic habitat is home to some of the strangest sharks, chiefly spiny-finned species from the Squaliformes group (see page 50). In some regions, where food is plentiful, they are so common that they form the largest component of the biomass (the mass or weight of all living things) in that habitat. Bramble sharks dwell below 1,600 feet. Frilled sharks and six- and seven-gilled sharks do the same. They feed on carrion floating down from above, or on other bottom-dwelling creatures such as shellfish and worms. Having no need for speed or stamina, they are among the slowest of all sharks.

above right: **A mako shark trails strings of
eggs of the parasites called copepods, sea-living
crustacean cousins of the humble pond water-
flea (see page 77).**

Do Sharks Grow Old?

MOST LARGE ANIMALS GROW TO ADULT SIZE IN A FEW YEARS, THEN STOP. EVEN ELEPHANTS, WHALES, AND CROCODILES ARE ALMOST FULLY GROWN IN ABOUT 10–15 YEARS.

Some bony fish, like goldfish, grow rapidly and then slow down. Their adult size is partly related to the amount of room they have, and their food supply.

Sharks, on the other hand, grow much more slowly. Even small species can take many years to reach full size. Growth rates in cold conditions are generally slower throughout the living world, although of course there are exceptions. Sharks from colder waters grow slowly, because the chemical processes inside their bodies are retarded in the lower temperatures. If food is plentiful, a shark grows slightly more rapidly. If food is scarce, it may not grow at all.

how to age a shark

Assessing lifespans for wild animals is famously difficult. Accurate measurements for sharks kept in aquaria are one method, but this is hardly a natural habitat. In the wild, catch-and-release and tagging projects can give clues to lifespans and growth rates.

Bony fish have skin scales with "rings," like those in a tree trunk, which can indicate age. But sharks do not. Their skin denticles grow, wear, fall out, and are replaced throughout life.

Some young sharks differ from their parents, not only in size. They may live in shallower water, feed on smaller prey, have smaller, differently shaped teeth, and vary in their skin colors and markings. Their ages can sometimes be estimated from these changes in appearance.

growth rates

In aquaria, young and healthy sharks with plentiful food grow about six inches longer each year. This is much slower than comparable bony fish. In the wild, sharks probably grow much more slowly. One tagged great white had lengthened less than half an inch each year. A re-caught Greenland shark had grown only a fifth of an inch per year.

The fastest-growing species are the large ocean hunters, when food is abundant. Blues and makos may lengthen by eight inches or more yearly in such favorable conditions. This faster growth rate is probably due partly to their higher body temperatures (see page 64). It also needs food input equivalent to 1·5–3 percent of the shark's body weight, every day.

below: **Decades of growth make fish this big. This whale shark is being freed from a fishing net by divers in the Red Sea.**

70

ECOLOGY AND BIOLOGY

So a large great white, weighing just over a ton, requires 11 tons of food in one year.

why grow so slowly?

One reason for the low growth rate of sharks is their slow digestive systems. Most species probably eat only every two or three days. Some can fast for several months, surviving on fat reserves in the huge liver.

Slow growth also means slow reproduction, since sexual maturity is related more to body length than to age. Larger species do not breed until about 10 feet in length, which could take 15 years to achieve.

SOME RIPE OLD AGES

Most sharks are thought to live for about 25 years, as a good maximum average in the wild. Bigger ones probably live longer. Results of tagging experiments include:

• Australian school shark—at least 34 years.
• Great white—at least 25 years.
• Greenland shark—at least 16 years.

Other estimates include:
• Whale shark—about 70 years.
• Piked dogfish—possibly 100 years.

Sharks on the Move

Sharks move long distances, or migrate, to exploit new food sources, to avoid danger—especially other sharks—or to find mates (see page 170).

seasonal patterns

Many animals, from butterflies to whales, migrate to find food. Sharks are no exception. Numerous species move seasonally, following the migrations of their food items such as fish, squid, small whales and seals. These creatures, in turn, follow their own food.

The overall pattern of seasonal migration can be traced back to the base of the food web, the plankton. This grows fast or "blooms" in the nutrient-rich polar seas during the short summer. It also thrives in temperate seas and wherever currents well up from deep water. As a result of this many animals head from tropical and temperate regions to the far north and

south, to take advantage of it. In winter, the polar waters are too cold and dark, so they head back to the tropics. The waters there support less plankton growth, because they are poorer in nutrients, but the growth is more constant through the year.

Thresher and blue sharks follow this pattern in the Atlantic. They are found in warmer waters in winter, and migrate north as far as the North Sea in summer.

a mystery solved?

One of the plankton-feeding sharks is the huge basking shark. It is seen in large schools in the summer, in many oceans. But in winter, when the food supply is scarce, it is mysteriously absent. In 1953, several individuals were caught at the start of winter. They had shed their gill rakers, which filter the plankton (see page 148). It was thought that they might sink to the

above: **To us, most whitetip reef sharks look very similar! This perceived lack of individuality is a further limit on our studies of shark movements and migrations.**

opposite above: **Only certain sharks, like the relatively slow and docile Port Jacksons, are amenable to having tags clipped to their fins or bodies.**

ECOLOGY AND BIOLOGY

72

bottom in winter, and save energy by hibernating until spring. Was this the answer? The story has yet to be proved.

Megamouth sharks are also filter-feeders. Their migrations are also vertical, but daily, not yearly. At night they swim up from the depths toward mid-water, to meet shrimp feeding on plankton that are coming down from the surface. By day the plankton comes back up to the sunlit upper waters, while the megamouths sink to the depths and rest.

Requiem and hammerhead sharks travel long distances daily, as well as seasonally, possibly in search of rich hunting grounds. Tagged blue sharks have clocked up distances of 1,430 miles from their original catch site. Spiny dogfish have been found up to 5,000 miles away from where they were tagged, eight years previously.

below: **Despite their huge bulk, basking sharks can soon disappear into the cloudy gloom of the sea. This makes visual tracking very difficult.**

STAYING SAFE

Lemon sharks are born in shallow bays and lagoons. They spend their first two years here hiding among the seaweed, feeding on small fish, and staying away from other sharks—including their own parents, who are more offshore. The youngsters graduate into slightly deeper water between the ages of three and five years, then to deep-water reefs as they reach adulthood.

Do Sharks Have Friends?

IT SEEMS UNLIKELY THAT OTHER CREATURES WOULD WILLINGLY COME NEAR A LARGE AND HUNGRY SHARK. BUT TWO TYPES OF FISH ARE OFTEN FOUND WITH SHARKS, AND A THIRD MAKES REGULAR VISITS—FOR REASONS OF HYGIENE.

stuck to a shark

The various species of shark-suckers, also called remoras, are slim fish varying from about eight inches to just over three feet in length. They have bold black-and-white stripes, and dorsal fins modified into large oval suckers. The two halves of the fin form louver-like ridges, with a raised rim around the outside. When the rim is put against a surface, and the louvers lowered, this creates a vacuum inside, and the surrounding water pressure forces the sucker against the surface.

Remoras can suck on to a shark with a force that would support 22 pounds. They also attach themselves to other large fish, turtles, whales and even ships.

showing the way

Another fish that often accompanies sharks is the pilot fish. About four feet long, it has spines along its back and vertical body stripes. The Ancient Greeks believed pilot fish could guide ships to land. They certainly swim alongside ships, and also whales, sharks, and other large creatures, sometimes for many days.

They save energy by keeping close to the bigger animal, "slip-streaming" within the boundary layer of water that it drags along as it swims. Using another animal for transport in this way is called phoresy.

why stay close?

Scientists are unsure as to why remoras and pilot fish stay near their hosts. It was once thought that the keen-eyed pilots could guide their companions to large prey, and then feast on the left-overs and scraps. But most large hunting sharks have good eyesight of their

own. Also, the pilot's stomach contents are mainly whole small fish, not leftover scraps.

Sharks and other fish who live around coral reefs often visit a particular place on the reef. This is a cleaning station and the cleaner is a type of fish, a small finger-sized wrasse. Huge sharks, barracudas, groupers, and other fearsome giants allow the little cleaner to enter their mouths and gill slits, and pick off dead skin and scales, small parasitic animals like lice, also barnacles, fungi, growths, and other debris. The cleaners do have distinct patterns and dances but it is still not clear how these inhibit the "killer instinct" of the larger fish.

above: **A boldly-striped shark-sucker accompanies a zebra shark on its travels.**

ECOLOGY AND BIOLOGY

above: **On Australia's
Great Barrier Reef,
small pilot fish stay
just in front of the
tawny nurse shark's
mouth—riding the
bow wave?**

left: **A tiny goby
cleans a whitetip reef
shark near Cocos
Island, Costa Rica.
(The cleaner fish is
near the shark's
right nostril.)**

E C O L O G Y   A N D   B I O L O G Y

Do Sharks Have Enemies?

IN MOST ECOSYSTEMS, THE TOP PREDATORS ARE SO BIG AND FIERCE THAT THEY HAVE FEW NATURAL ENEMIES. THIS APPLIES TO SHARKS.

The shark's main threats are larger sharks, big hunting mammals such as porpoises and dolphins, and killer and sperm whales. Plus the unnatural and universal enemy—humans.

Many shark species have the defense of sheer size. Whale and basking sharks, though inoffensive, are simply too big to tackle. Most other shark species grow to over three feet in length. The average size of bony fish is 4–12 inches. The other major type of numerous predator in the sea, squid, are not much larger. These rarely present a danger to sharks.

the shark menaced

Porpoises are known to attack a large shark in self-defense. They surround it and ram it in turn from the sides, until it retreats. Dolphins are also known to ram sharks, especially on their sensitive gills or cloacal region—the genital and excretory area. Some seals have scars that indicate they escaped from a shark.

The killer whale, bigger than a great white, is an intelligent, fearsome, powerful, pack-hunting predator. Most animals in the sea avoid it, including sharks—an average-sized species

above: **Dolphins are not known for their friendliness to sharks. They are potential shark victims, and may ram or bite the enemy.**

would make a nice-sized snack. Playing the tape-recorded sounds of killer whales to bull sharks causes the shark great agitation. The tables turned.

the enemies within

Threatening animals do not have to be big and fierce. Like other living things, sharks are unwilling hosts to parasites that live on and inside them, feeding on their tissues.

Sleeper sharks often have parasitic copepods (small crustaceans resembling woodlice or water-fleas) attached to their eyes. The parasite does considerable damage to the cornea, the domed, transparent front of the eye. Even uninfested sharks have scar tissue on the cornea, from past parasitic attack. This must impede vision, but sleeper sharks are slow-swimming bottom-dwellers in dark waters, so they probably do not depend on eyesight to any great degree.

Like the great whales, big sharks may be dotted with firmly fixed skin parasites such as barnacles, lice, and copepods. Whale sharks may rub themselves against boats, apparently itching to get rid of the unwelcome guests. Basking sharks leap from the water, possibly trying to relieve the irritation.

worms in the gut

Sharks are also host to tapeworms, which live within their digestive system. The worm hangs on to the lining of the gut with its tiny hooked head, and absorbs the nutrients all around it, through its thin, moist skin.

Tapeworms produce bags of eggs at their rear ends, which detach and pass out with the shark's feces (droppings). Like tapeworms on land, they have complicated life cycles that involve other hosts in addition to the shark.

inset below: **Copepods cling to the underside of a hammerhead shark's snout. They are external, or ecto-parasites.**

below: **The killer whale eats almost anything it chooses. This varies from young sea-lions to medium-sized sharks.**

Breathing Underwater

ALMOST ALL LIVING THINGS NEED OXYGEN. THIS SUBSTANCE IS A VITAL PART OF THE CHEMICAL PROCESS CALLED CELLULAR RESPIRATION, INSIDE THE BODY'S MICROSCOPIC CELLS AND TISSUES, WHICH RELEASES ENERGY FROM DIGESTED FOOD TO DRIVE LIFE PROCESSES.

above: **Bony fish such as the kingfish have gills very similar to those of sharks. But a bony flap, the gill cover or operculum, protects and hides the gills and their slits.**

Humans breathe oxygen-containing air into our lungs. Sharks, like other aquatic creatures, depend on oxygen dissolved in water. They extract it with specialized body parts—gills. Water comes in through the mouth, flows over the gills, and out through the gill slits.

the structure of gills

Most fish, including the majority of sharks, have five pairs of gill openings on the sides of the head. Most sharks also have a sixth gill opening, in the form of a small hole or spiracle.

In a shark, each arch-shaped gill is supported by a cartilage bar which curves around the side of the throat cavity. This arch carries a double-fringe of hundreds of feathery-looking gill filaments. In turn, each filament is made of thousands of tiny leaflike branches: lamellae. This design creates a very large surface area for absorbing as much oxygen as possible.

how gills work

The delicate, thin-walled lamellae contain microscopic thin-walled blood vessels: capillaries. As blood flows through these, it is very close to the water outside. Oxygen seeps or diffuses from its relatively high concentration in the water, to the lower concentration in the blood. One of the shark body's waste products, carbon dioxide, passes in the opposite direction, from blood out into the water.

The efficiency of the system is improved by the countercurrent principle. Water flows over the gills from front to back. Blood flows within the gills from back to front. This produces an appreciable difference at all parts of the gill between the concentrations of oxygen in water, where it is higher, and blood, where it is lower, to encourage its transfer.

constant flow

Gills need a constant supply of new water In some sharks, muscular action draws water into the mouth, shuts the mouth, and squeezes the water over the gills, out through the gill slits, as more water is sucked into the mouth. Valves prevent water going down the throat, and gill flaps stop it coming in through the gill slits.

To aid this pumped flow, most sharks swim forwards all the time. If they cannot—for example, if they are trapped in a net—they get into severe breathing difficulties and oxygen shortage. The open-ocean hunting sharks depend almost entirely on their forward motion, for buoyancy as well as for maintaining their breathing. They do not use the pumping mechanism described above. If they cannot swim, they sink and suffocate.

variations on the theme

Bottom-living sharks like the wobbegong do not keep swimming, and they also risk blocking their gills with debris stirred up from the sea bed. So they have a modified system, breathing in through their spiracle holes and out through gill slits, like skates and rays.

The Port Jackson shark, another bottom-dweller, has a different modification. It pumps water in through its first pair of gill slits and out over the other four.

Whale and basking sharks use their massive gills for breathing, and also as plankton-filters for feeding (see page 148).

above: **The seven-gilled shark, *Notorhynchus maculatis*, displays its extra gill slits.**

left: **A close-up view of the gill slits of the dusky shark. The gills themselves are hidden just beneath.**

MORE OF LESS

• Fresh air contains about 21 percent gaseous oxygen.

• Our lungs can extract about one-quarter of this oxygen.

• Surface sea water contains only 1 percent dissolved oxygen, and this proportion reduces to less than 0.025 percent in deep water.

• Fish gills can extract some four-fifths of this dissolved oxygen.

The Shark's Lifeblood

BLOOD IS AN AMAZING FLUID. IT DISTRIBUTES THROUGHOUT THE BODY VITAL SUBSTANCES SUCH AS OXYGEN, NUTRIENTS, AND VITAMINS AND MINERALS FROM DIGESTED FOOD HORMONES FOR COORDINATING INNER PROCESSES, DISEASE-FIGHTING ANTIBODIES, AND MUCH MORE.

It also collects bodily wastes and by-products for removal.

The blood transport system is such a successful design that it is used by invertebrates and vertebrates alike, including sharks. Their blood is pumped by the heart through a system of tubes called blood vessels (see page 82).

plasma and cells

Shark blood is fairly typical, for a vertebrate. It consists of a straw-colored liquid, plasma, in which microscopic cells float. Plasma is a watery solution of hundreds of body chemicals, salts, nutrients, hormones, and wastes.

There are two main kinds of blood cells, or corpuscles. Red blood cells contain a red-colored substance, haemoglobin, which has a strong attachment for oxygen. There are millions of red cells in just one drop of blood, and their job is to absorb oxygen in the gills, and give it up to the tissues around the body.

The second kind of blood cells, white cells, help to protect the body against diseases and infections. Some of the white cells simply engulf and "eat" any foreign or unfamiliar matter that gets into the body, including bacteria and other germs. Other white cells make substances called antibodies, which attach to and destroy invading germs.

hormones and lymph

The shark's hormone or endocrine system consists of many glands throughout the body. They include the pituitary in the brain, the thymus, thyroid, and parathyroid glands in the "neck" region, the two-part adrenal glands near the kidneys, and the sex glands—ovaries in

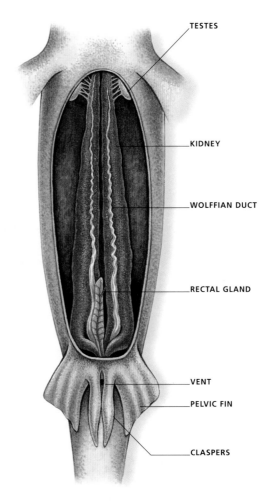

TESTES

KIDNEY

WOLFFIAN DUCT

RECTAL GLAND

VENT

PELVIC FIN

CLASPERS

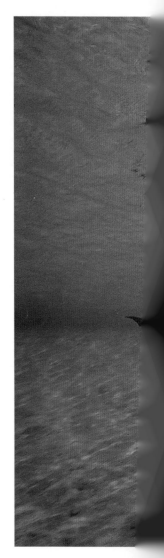

left: **A diagram of the sexual and excretory (urogenital) organs of a male shark. The paired kidneys run along either side of the dorsal surface of the abdominal cavity.**

the female, testes in the male. These glands make chemical messengers called hormones, which circulate in the blood and control many of the shark's inner body processes, such as using energy, removing wastes, growth, and sexual maturation.

Vertebrates such as sharks have a second transport fluid in the body: lymph. This consists of general body fluids in the tissues, blood that "leaks" out of its vessels, and liquids that ooze out of microscopic cells. Lymph flows slowly through a fine network of open channels and tubes, propelled mainly by the squeezing motions of body muscles as the shark moves. It collects in bigger tubes and eventually empties back into the veins of the main blood system. Lymph assists blood by delivering nutrients, collecting wastes, and fighting infections.

below: **A tiger shark swishes through the clear shallows, leaving a trail of invisible wastes, including carbon dioxide from the blood. This is passed out in dissolved form, via the gills, into the water.**

HOT STUFF

Most fish are cold-blooded. More accurately, they are poikilothermic. Their body temperature is almost the same as the surrounding water. But the mackerel shark group, including the great white, mako, porbeagle, and thresher, are warm-blooded, or homeothermic. They maintain a higher, relatively constant body temperature compared with the water, sometimes 45–50°F above ambient water temperature. The only other large animals that do this are birds and mammals. The heat is produced by muscle activity and biochemical reactions in the tissues, and spread around the body by the blood. Homeothermy allows a creature to be more active and move faster than the colder creatures around it—but it also uses up more energy, which must be taken in as extra food.

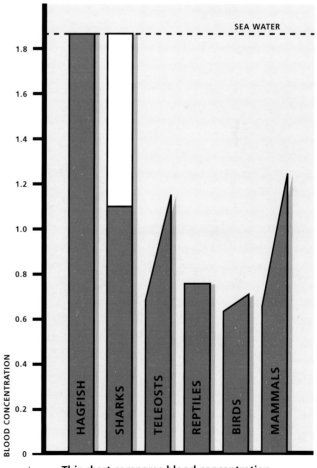

above: **This chart compares blood concentration in various animals. Shark and hagfish blood is very concentrated. In sharks urea salts (shown in white) contribute greatly to blood concentration.**

Sharks Have a Heart

THE SHARK'S HEART IS THE PUMP FOR ITS BLOOD CIRCULATORY SYSTEM.

BEING A VERY ANCIENT GROUP, SHARKS HAVE A SLIGHTLY DIFFERENT DESIGN

OF HEART, COMPARED WITH OTHER VERTEBRATES.

below right: **No sign of outward activity, but in its "neck", the heart of this endormi shark beats steadily to circulate blood.**

below: **The blood vessels which carry the nutrients from the yolk sacs of these young spurdog embryos are clearly visible.**

In ourselves, the heart is a double pump and blood has a double circulation. It goes to the lungs to gather oxygen, back to the heart, then around the body to deliver oxygen, and back to the heart. In sharks, blood goes from the heart to the gills to gather oxygen, then onward around the body to deliver the oxygen, before returning to the heart.

from the heart

The heart itself is just behind the shark's lower jaw. It is effectively a thickened part of the main blood vessel, the aorta, folded back on itself and divided into four chambers. The walls are composed of strong muscle which contracts rhythmically, compressing the blood within, and pushing it along. Valves in the chambers make the blood flow one way only, on a steady and never-ending circuit, through the system of blood vessels.

Vessels that carry blood away from the heart are arteries. They have thick, muscular walls that bulge or pulse with the pressurized surge of blood from each heartbeat.

The main artery, the ventral aorta, carries low-oxygen blood from the heart, directly to the gills. Here it divides into five branched pairs, one for each gill arch. Each branch divides more and more, into microscopic, thin-walled blood vessels, capillaries, within the gill filaments. Oxygen passes from the water into these. Coming away from the gills, the capillaries join and become wider, finally forming another large artery, the dorsal aorta. Like the ventral

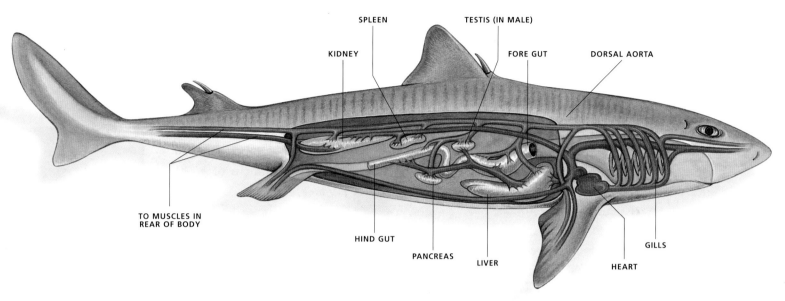

SPLEEN   TESTIS (IN MALE)

KIDNEY   FORE GUT   DORSAL AORTA

TO MUSCLES IN
REAR OF BODY

HIND GUT   GILLS

PANCREAS

LIVER   HEART

aorta, the dorsal aorta divides and branches into smaller arteries that convey blood to all of the body. The arteries divide repeatedly to form capillaries, thinner than hairs. Their walls are so thin that oxygen, nutrients, and other substances can pass out into the tissues. Wastes and by-products pass the other way, from the tissues into the blood.

back to the heart

Capillaries join together into larger tubes, veins and even larger sinuses or spaces. The vein network carries blood back to the heart. Since this blood has passed through at least two, even three, capillary systems, it has lost its high pressure and pulse. So vein walls, unlike artery walls, are thin and floppy.

The veins and sinuses empty into two vessels. These, together with a pair of hepatic veins from the liver, empty in turn into the first chamber of the heart, the sinus venosus. From here the blood passes into the second chamber, the auricle or atrium, and is then sucked into the third chamber, the thick-walled ventricle. This provides the main power to force the blood into the fourth chamber, a valved bulb called the conus arteriosus, at the base of the main artery. From here it passes back out into the ventral aorta.

sub-circuits

In most of the shark's circulatory system, arteries split into capillaries in the gills, which come together as arteries for the body, which split into more capillaries, that come together as veins for return to the heart. But in parts of the body, there is yet another stage to the circuit. Such arrangements are called portal systems.

In the hepatic portal system, blood from the intestines passes along veins—not back to the heart, but through the liver first. The renal portal system carries blood from the tail end of the shark, along veins that lead through the kidneys first, before returning it to the heart.

above: **Blood circulates around the shark's body in tube-like blood vessels. It receives oxygen in the gills and passes to the muscles and body organs, then back to the heart.**

SHARK HEART—PUMP AND SUCK

The heart of a shark or other elasmobranch not only pumps blood out under forceful pressure, as its muscular walls contract and squeeze. When the heart relaxes between beats, it also actively sucks blood in from the veins. This happens because the heart is encased in a fairly rigid box-like chamber, the pericardium. As the heart itself contracts and becomes smaller, it causes the pericardium to collapse inwards, like sucking in your own cheeks. This produces a low pressure inside the pericardial chamber, allowing blood flow in from the veins to refill the heart. So the shark's heart is both a pressure pump and suction pump.

SEA WATER HAS A RELATIVELY HIGH CONCENTRATION OF SALTS SUCH AS SODIUM AND CHLORIDE. SIMILARLY, THE BODY FLUIDS INSIDE AN ANIMAL ALSO CONTAIN DISSOLVED SALTS AND OTHER SUBSTANCES.

If these two sets of salts are unbalanced or unequal in concentration, this causes problems, due to osmosis. This is the natural tendency for concentrations to even out, by water passing from the weaker solution to the stronger one, and/or by salts passing the other way.

This is the area of biology called osmoregulation. It is closely linked to the process of filtering and removing wastes from the body, which is known as excretion.

fresh—or salted ...

Fish that live in fresh water face one aspect of the problem. Their body fluids are more concentrated than the surrounding water, so the water tends to enter them, by osmosis. Thick skin helps to minimize this effect. But water still comes in through the mouth lining, guts, and especially through the gills, which have thin and delicate coverings so they can absorb oxygen. Freshwater fish solve the problem by their kidneys excreting huge amounts of very dilute urine, which contains this copious extra water.

Sea-water fish have the reverse problem. Their fluids and tissues are less concentrated than the salty water around them. So water tends to leave their bodies.

The bony fish's answer is to drink large amounts of sea water. This takes in the extra required water—and extra salts, too. So their kidneys make small amounts of very concentrated urine, getting rid of the salts and wastes, but not much water.

the shark's solution

Sharks have yet another answer. They effectively avoid the problem of osmoregulation, by keeping their body fluids and tissues at the same concentration as the surrounding sea water, or even slightly higher. This is achieved by maintaining high concentrations of waste products, especially urea, in the blood. We have urea in our blood, and our kidneys filter it out as urine. Sharks do the same (see page 86). But the concentration of urea and another waste, trimethylamine oxide, in their blood, tissue fluids, and urine is much greater. This is why some captured sharks, such as the Greenland shark, smell strongly of uncleaned human toilets!

Sharks, skates and rays, hagfish, coelacanths, and lungfish are the only vertebrates that recycle and reabsorb urea into their blood, in this way. These are all very ancient groups, so it must have been an early answer to the problem of osmoregulation for aquatic animals.

above: **The bull shark has surprised and attacked people in the entirely fresh water of rivers and lakes.**

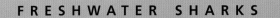

FRESHWATER SHARKS

Several shark species, such as tiger sharks, can enter the brackish (partly salty) water of river mouths, for brief feeding visits. But only the bull sharks can truly live in fresh water. Also known as Zambesi sharks or Lake Nicaragua sharks, they are found hundreds of miles up tropical rivers in Africa and South America. They cope with fresh water by lowering the urea content of their tissues, and removing the excess water that enters the body via their kidneys, as very dilute urine.

below: A shark such as this silvertip is surrounded by a relatively concentrated cocktail of dissolved salts—sea water. This causes problems for body fluids.

Shark Kidneys

IN SHARKS AND OTHER VERTEBRATES, MOST OF THE BY-PRODUCTS AND WASTES COLLECTED FROM THE TISSUES BY THE BLOOD ARE FILTERED BY THE KIDNEYS.

Along with excess water, and various unwanted minerals and salts, they go to make the liquid waste called urine.

A shark's two kidneys are long and narrow, lying on either side of the vertebral column, approximately under the dorsal fin. Like our own kidneys, they consist of many microscopic tubes, called renal tubules, closely intertwined with the tiny blood vessels known as capillaries. The walls of both tubules and capillaries are one cell thick, and these cells are specially adapted to regulate the passage of salts and water through themselves.

Each kidney contains hundreds of units called renal corpuscles. A renal corpuscle has one end of the tubule which is expanded into a cup shape, the Bowman's capsule. This surrounds a knotlike bundle of blood capillaries, the glomerulus.

The renal corpuscles of sharks are among the largest of any vertebrate—many times bigger than those in our own kidneys, in order to deal with the excess water.

wanted and unwanted

In the renal corpuscle, water and dissolved substances from the blood in the capillaries are "squeezed" into the cup-shaped end of the tubule, and along its microscopically twisting, tortuous length. Cells lining the tubule allow certain desirable substances to pass out of the tubule, back into the surrounding fluids and blood vessels. Unwanted wastes and water stay in the tubule.

A specialized part of the tubule, found only in sharks, skates, and rays, also returns precisely regulated amounts of two wastes, urea and trimethylamine oxide, to the blood. This is part of the osmoregulation system (see page 84).

out into the sea

The hundreds of tubules in each kidney join together at their ends into five urinary ducts. These carry the body's fluid waste contents, urine, into a urinary sinus—the shark's bladder. The sinuses from both kidneys join to the dual-purpose opening for excretion and reproduction, the cloaca. From here, the urine is voided into the sea.

As a shark's body fluids and tissues are balanced in concentration with the sea water, sharks produce very little urine for their size. A human-sized shark would make perhaps one-tenth of the amount of urine an average human being makes.

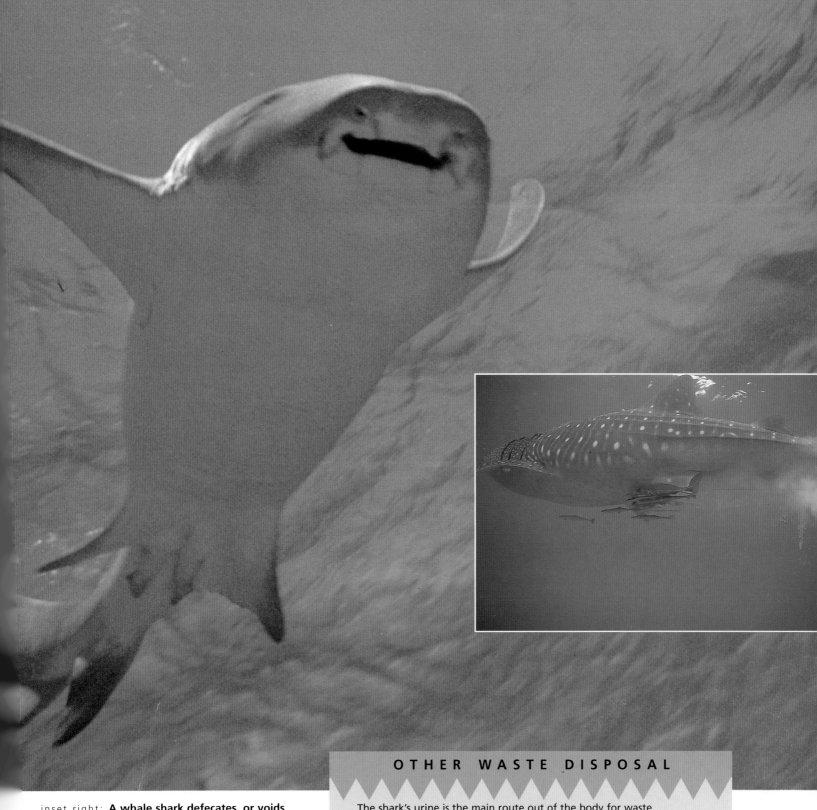

inset right: **A whale shark defecates, or voids its digestive wastes, as a huge cloud into the waters of Ningaloo Reef, Western Australia.**

above: **The rear body opening or cloaca, just in front of the pelvic fins, is used as an exit for kidney-filtered urine, digestive feces, and reproductive sperm or eggs.**

opposite left: **The sea cucumber is one of many creatures that sifts sand and mud on the seabed, taking in edible particles from the droppings of sharks and other animals.**

OTHER WASTE DISPOSAL

The shark's urine is the main route out of the body for waste substances and by-products from the cells and tissues. But there are other waste systems, too.

- Some unwanted salts and minerals, along with carbon dioxide, pass through the thin, delicate gills, into the water.

- Wastes from undigestible and undigested food pass to the end of the gut and out through the cloaca, as feces (droppings).

- The liver breaks down old blood cells and other items, and mixes their remains with digestive juices to make bile. This yellowish fluid is stored in the gall bladder, squeezed into the guts to help with digestion, and eventually voided with the feces.

CHAPTER 4

Sense and Supersense

Sense-ational Sharks

SHARKS HAVE THE SAME FIVE MAIN SENSES AS HUMANS—SIGHT, HEARING, TOUCH, TASTE, AND SMELL. BUT THEY LIVE IN THE TOTALLY DIFFERENT WORLD OF THE AQUATIC ENVIRONMENT.

Sharks have no distinction, as we do on land, between airborne smells and waterborne tastes, although there is evidence of some sharks sniffing the air. Everything is in water.

Their detecting organs are very different, in threshold levels and sensitivity, from our own. They also have senses that we cannot relate to, like the ability to detect currents and ripples in the water, tiny electrical pulses and, perhaps, magnetic fields. And the shark's brain works in a very different way than our own. So sharks must experience sensations we simply cannot imagine, in ways we cannot comprehend.

tuned to the environment

Like all creatures, sharks have senses to find out about the world around them, to detect food, to locate a mate at breeding time, and to avoid danger and harsh conditions. Over millions of years, evolution has fine-tuned these senses to the watery habitat in which they live and each species' way of life.

Our own senses are dominated by sight. But light does not travel well through sea water, and soon fades with a few yards' depth. So sharks rely on other cues. Sounds and vibrations travel much faster and farther through water than through air. So do scented or smelly substances. Sharks are extremely sensitive to these stimuli, and use them instead of sight over long distances, especially when hunting.

As the food comes nearer, the shark probably brings vision into play. Then its amazing powers of electricity-detection tell it where to aim the bite. Finally, as the victim is between the teeth, the shark's close-contact senses, touch and taste, allow it to check the meal's suitability, before it is swallowed.

above: **Big eyes to see you with, both for the shark and its human admirer.**

previous page: **With eyes and nostrils on the tips of its "hammer", the hammerhead is extraordinarily sensitive to many features in its surroundings.**

where eyes are useless

Shark senses vary according to the habitat of each species. Sharks that live in the gloom of mid-water have proportionally large eyes, to gather what few light rays there are.

Those who dwell at depth, where the water is always inky-black and cold, have tiny eyes and poor vision. They probably use their senses of lateral line (ripples and currents) and physical touch to find their way along the contours of the sea bed.

They are also sensitive to sounds or long-distance vibrations, and to the electrical pulses given off by animal muscles. Detecting gravity and changes in water pressure tells them about depth, which way is up, and how to swim in a balanced, coordinated manner.

HOMING IN ON PREY

A typical shark probably uses its main senses in this order, as it tracks down a victim:

• Thousands of yards—sounds (vibrations in the water)

• Hundreds of yards—scents or smells

• Tens of yards—water ripples (lateral line)

• Yards—light (vision)

• Inches—electric sense

• Contact—taste, pressure, touch

below: **A nurse shark uses its battery of senses as it noses into the sand of the Florida Keys, searching for buried, hiding victims.**

The Shark's Brain

With the spinal cord, which is the main nerve projecting from it along the vertebral column, this makes up the central nervous system. The network of stringlike nerves that carry information between the central nervous system and the muscles and organs all over the body make up the peripheral system. Information is sent around in the form of coded patterns of tiny electrical pulses, called nerve signals.

Each nerve is made of hundreds or thousands of long but microscopically thin "wires," called nerve fibers or axons. These are parts of nerve cells or neurons. Those that carry nerve signals from the sense organs around the body to the spinal cord and brain are called sensory neurons. Their information is processed in the brain. In response, signals are sent out to the various muscles and organs by motor neurons, to make the shark move and react.

parts of the brain

The shark's brain is relatively simple, though basically similar to the brains of most other vertebrates. It has three main regions: the forebrain, midbrain, and hindbrain.

The forebrain consists mainly of bulges called olfactory lobes. These deal with information coming in from the smell and scent detectors. The part called the cerebrum is relatively small and involved mainly in processing this olfactory information. (In other vertebrates, especially birds and mammals, the cerebrum is the site of intelligence and learning. In ourselves, it makes up nine-tenths of the brain volume.)

The midbrain contains the optic lobes, which receive signals sent in from the eyes, concerning vision. It is also the region where most of the sensory information is coordinated, and from where instructions are sent out along motor nerves to the muscles, to control movements.

The hindbrain is comparatively large in all fish, including sharks. In the manner of an airplane's autopilot, it controls and coordinates basic life functions and motions, such as simple swimming, balance, heartbeat, blood pressure, digestion, and excretion.

right: **We may associate big eyes with an all-seeing, all-knowing outlook. But a shark's brain is proportionally very small and works on a completely different level from our own.**

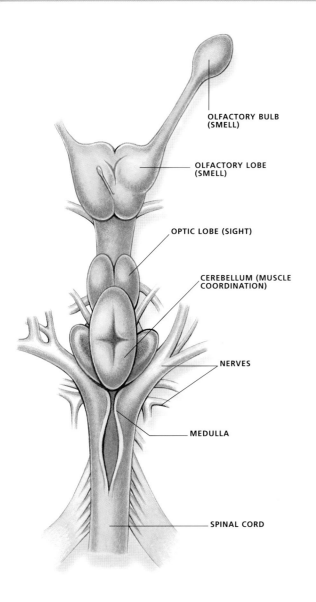

OLFACTORY BULB
(SMELL)

OLFACTORY LOBE
(SMELL)

OPTIC LOBE (SIGHT)

CEREBELLUM (MUSCLE
COORDINATION)

NERVES

MEDULLA

SPINAL CORD

BRAIN SIZE

The comparison of a creature's body size with its brain size might seem broadly to reflect what we term "intelligence." This involves learning and adaptable behavior. The brain–body ratios for some sharks is almost the same as for certain birds and mammals, around 1:1,000 or 1:500. (In ourselves, it is about 1:50.) However, much of the typical shark's brain is involved in analyzing the mass of information from its supersenses. The olfactory, optic, and other lobes are relatively large. The parts involved in learning and adaptation, such as the cerebrum, are relatively small.

below: **A side view of the brain shows how the shark's cerebrum is expanded into the two huge olfactory lobes, dealing with smell.**

above: **The brain of a shark, seen from above. The largest parts are concerned with smell, sight and coordination.**

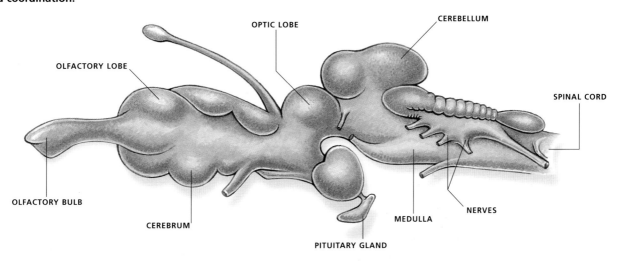

OPTIC LOBE

CEREBELLUM

OLFACTORY LOBE

SPINAL CORD

OLFACTORY BULB

CEREBRUM

PITUITARY GLAND

MEDULLA

NERVES

Super-scents

THE OCEAN IS FULL OF SCENTS AND SMELLS—FROM LIVING ANIMALS WHO RELEASE WASTES, HORMONES AND PHEROMONES (COMMUNICATING SUBSTANCES), THROUGH DEAD CREATURES AND PLANTS THAT DECAY AND ROT, TO GEOLOGICAL MINERALS AND SALTS DISSOLVING FROM THE ROCKS AND SEA BED, AND, INCREASINGLY, POLLUTION WITH OUR MANUFACTURED CHEMICALS.

The importance of smell in a shark's life is shown by the brain. The olfactory lobes which analyze smell information can make up to two-thirds of the brain's total weight.

site of smell

The olfactory organs that detect scents and smells are a pair of nasal sacs near the front of the shark's snout. Their openings are the shark's nostrils. In ourselves, nostrils are also an entrance to our breathing system. In most sharks, the nostrils are closed sacs and lead nowhere, used only for smell.

Each nasal sac is shaped so that water flows in, passes over the wrinkled inner surface, and flows out again, in a continuous stream as the shark swims. The wrinkled lining within the nostril is covered with microscopic cells. Some make a slimy mucus that coats the lining. Others are olfactory nerve cells. Each has a tuft of tiny microhairs which project from its upper surface, into the coating of mucus.

Smell-carrying substances in the water, called odorants, dissolve in the nasal mucus and stimulate these microhairs. This causes the olfactory nerve cells to send signals along nerves, which are contained within the olfactory bulb that surrounds the nasal sac.

The impulses are filtered and part-sorted in the olfactory bulb and also in the olfactory tract—the large bundle of nerves that conveys them to the olfactory lobe—at the front of the brain, for analysis and recognition.

what can sharks smell?

Shark smell is very discriminating. It cannot detect many substances at all, probably because these have little importance in the shark's life. But for significant smell odorants, produced by predators, prey, or mates, the shark is super-sensitive.

Experiments show that sharks respond most strongly to the body fluids and secretions of injured or distressed prey animals. If the same animals are healthy and uninjured, the shark reacts less strongly, and it soon loses interest. Blood is very high on the list, causing responses at concentrations of only one part in one million—that is, about one pinhead-sized drop in a bathtub of water, or one teaspoonful in an average swimming pool. Some experts say that some sharks are 100 times more sensitive even than this.

Tales of sharks swimming unerringly towards a prey from 12 or so miles' distance are probably exaggerated. A reasonably large injured animal,

left: **An epaulette shark inches across the Great Barrier Reef, detecting a vast array of scents that we can hardly begin to imagine.**

SENSE AND SUPERSENSE

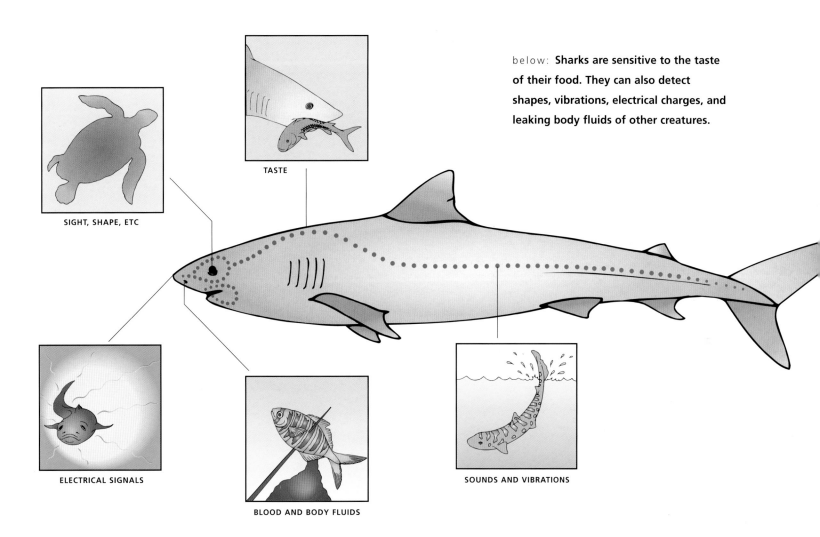

SIGHT, SHAPE, ETC

TASTE

below: **Sharks are sensitive to the taste of their food. They can also detect shapes, vibrations, electrical charges, and leaking body fluids of other creatures.**

ELECTRICAL SIGNALS

BLOOD AND BODY FLUIDS

SOUNDS AND VIBRATIONS

like a wounded seal, might attract sharks from a mile or a little more. They home in by following the increasing strength of the scent trail in the water. As it swims, the shark swings its head from side to side and swims continuously from side to side across the odor trail in order to climb the gradient. Its brain compares the strength of the smell in each nostril, and keeps turning toward the side where this is stronger. A larger distance between the nostrils would improve this direction-finding, and may be one reason for the hammerhead shark's strange-shaped head (see page 102).

TASTE

Sharks have microscopic taste buds scattered around the lining of the mouth and throat. Each taste bud is like a minute rounded cave in the lining, with a narrow opening or mouth on the surface. Inside are spindle-shaped gustatory sensory cells. Like the tufty-hair olfactory nerve cells of smell, these gustatory nerve cells respond to certain chemicals dissolved in the water, which seep through the taste bud's entrance. The gustatory nerve cells send nerve signals along the gustatory nerve to the brain.

Like us, sharks can discriminate only a few basic flavors, such as bitter, sweet, salty, and sour. Some bottom-living species have whisker-like barbels that bear taste buds, to "taste" the seabed. Most sharks lack taste buds in the skin of other parts of their bodies, which many bony fish possess.

Visionary Sharks

THE SHARK'S EYE IS TYPICAL OF MOST VERTEBRATES, INCLUDING OURSELVES. THE JELLY-FILLED

EYEBALL IS PROTECTED IN A SOCKET, OR ORBIT, IN THE SKULL.

above: **A smooth dogfish peers through the gloom, one eye tilted around to view the camera. This exposes the eyeball's whitish protective sheath, the sclera.**

At the front of the eyeball is a transparent "window"—the cornea. Light passes through this, through a hole called the pupil in a ring of muscle known as the iris, through a hard, ball-shaped lens, through the clear jelly within the eyeball, and shines on to the light-sensitive layer on the rear eyeball lining: the retina.

Muscles that support the lens can move it forward or backward, to focus on distant or nearby objects. The iris muscles contract automatically, the brighter the light, to make the pupil smaller and protect the sensitive retina from overexposure. In some species this makes the pupil into a slit shape; in others it becomes a series of tiny holes.

rods and cones

In most sharks, the retina contains millions of microscopic rod cells. These are sensitive to light levels and send patterns of nerve signals along the optic nerve to the optic lobe of the brain. But rod cells cannot distinguish colors. So most sharks probably see grayish blurred shadows, rather than colorful details. A few sharks that live in clear waters have other light-sensitive retinal cells, called cones. These can pick out certain colors, though whether the shark perceives them in the way we do is not known.

Behind the retina is the tapetum, a layer of cells containing a silvery pigment. This works like a mirror to reflect any light that passes through the retina back into it for greater sensitivity. It also means the shark's eye appears to shine in the dark—like a cat's. Sharks have another device, too, unique among vertebrates. In very bright light, the tapetum can be covered with darkly pigmented cells. This cuts down its reflections and protects the sensitive retina.

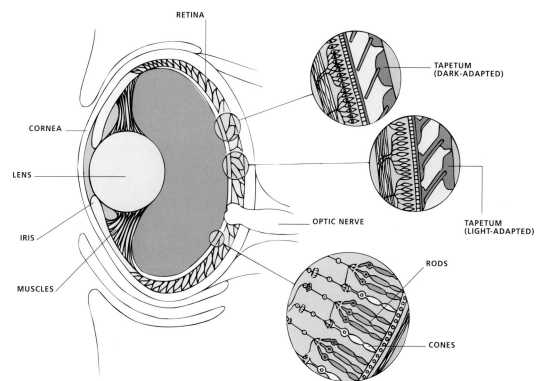

RETINA

TAPETUM
(DARK-ADAPTED)

CORNEA

LENS

IRIS

MUSCLES

OPTIC NERVE

TAPETUM
(LIGHT-ADAPTED)

RODS

CONES

right: **The structure of a shark's eye is basically similar to that of other vertebrates. The enlargements show the structure of the light-sensitive retina and the tapetum lucidum behind it.**

Sharks that live in gloomy mid-water have bigger eyes, to catch more light. The deep-sea thresher shark's eyes are the size of human fists.

eyes on the sides

Most sharks have eyes on the sides of the head, facing outward rather than to the front. They can see forward and backward, even up and down, at the same time. But an area of overlap in the views from the two eyes is very rare in sharks. This means they cannot judge distances well by sight, using binocular or stereoscopic vision, as we can with our forward-facing eyes.

A typical shark has upper and lower eyelids, to close and protect the eyeball. But the two eyelids do not usually meet. Instead, a third eyelid—the nictitating membrane—is drawn across the eye for protection. Some sharks close this at the moment of biting. Other sharks lack the nictitating membrane. So when they bite, they roll their eyeballs up under their true upper eyelids, giving a white-eyed appearance. The skaamoog or shy-eye shark is so named because it curls its tail over its eyes when caught.

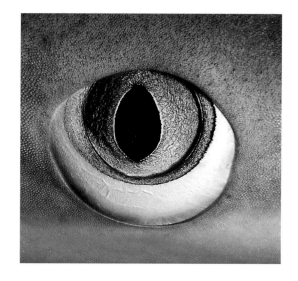

left: **The "black patch" in a shark's eye is the pupil, the hole through which light enters, just as in our own eyes. This one is slit-shaped, as in cats.**

THE "THIRD EYE"

In most vertebrates, including fish, amphibians, and reptiles, there is a "third eye" in the middle of the forehead, called the pineal body. Its is not a true eye, more a patch of light-sensitive cells under thin skin. It detects overall light levels and works as part of the hormonal system, for example, to control changing skin color in bottom-living sharks who use camouflage to blend in with the background.

The Sounds of the Sea

THE SEAS ARE FULL OF SOUND—SWISHING WATER CURRENTS, PASSING CREATURES SUCH AS

FISH AND SQUID, WAVES SPLASHING AT THE SURFACE AND SHORE, SINGING WHALES,

GRUNTING SEALS, AND, INCREASINGLY, SHIP ENGINES AND CHURNING PROPELLERS.

above: **What looks like the "ear" of this nurse shark is in fact its spiracle, an opening for water, related to the gill system. The"ear" is under the skin.**

Sharks detect sounds with two sets of sensory organs: the ears and the lateral line system (see page 100).

In the sea, sounds and vibrations travel as ripples of water pressure. Both the ears and lateral line detect these using sets of microscopic sensors called mechanoreceptors. A mechano-receptor has a group of sensory nerve cells, each bearing a tuft of hairs. These are embedded in a solid jelly lump called the cupola, whose move-ment is affected by pressures and movements in the outside water. As the jelly lump sways in

vibrations and currents, it bends the hairs, and this stimulates their nerve cells to send signals to the brain.

shark ears

The shark's ears are two tiny holes positioned on the sides of its head, behind the eyes. Each leads along a narrow tube to the inner ear, a fluid-filled cavity on the outside of the back of the skull. The inner ear consists of a series of connected tubes, called a labyrinth, which are themselves filled with fluid.

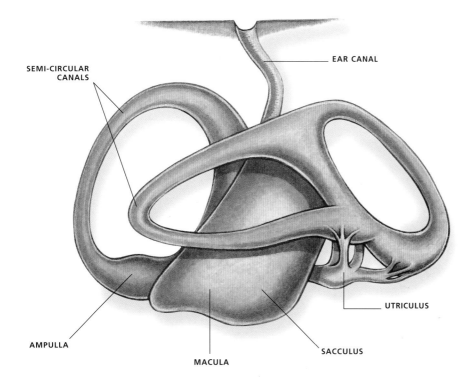

SEMI-CIRCULAR
CANALS

EAR CANAL

UTRICULUS

AMPULLA

MACULA

SACCULUS

left: **The inner ear of the shark, like that of other vertebrates, is not just concerned with hearing. The semi-circular canals are also organs of balance.**

The labyrinth's lining contains clusters of mechanoreceptors, as described above. Their microhairs are stimulated by movements of the nearby otoliths, which are tiny, stony lumps suspended in the fluid around them.

Parts of the labyrinth are involved in balance (see panel). The lower part, the sacculus, is concerned with hearing. Since the shark's flesh has a similar density to that of sea water, the pressure waves and vibrations of sounds pass not only along the fine tubes to the inner ears, but also straight through the shark's head, which is, in effect, acoustically transparent. The waves strike the much denser, stony otoliths in the inner ear and cause them to move, thereby stimulating nerve signals which are sent to the brain.

It's doubtful if sharks respond to a wide range of sounds, both in volume (loud or soft), and pitch or frequency (high or low), like we hear in air. Bull sharks react to sounds with a frequency of 20 to 1,000 Hz (cycles per second), which for us, would range from deep booms like

THE BALANCED APPROACH

The upper part of the shark's inner ear labyrinth is for balance. It consists of a chamber, the utriculus, and three C-shaped semicircular canals, each arranged at right angles to the other two. The linings of these chambers bear mechanoreceptors. As the shark leans, tilts, dives, and rises, the tiny, stonelike otoliths of the mechanoreceptors lag behind for a fraction of a second. Their swaying moves the nearby hairs of the sensory hair cells, and stimulates these cells to send signals to the brain. Combined with the inner sense of proprioception (see page 101), the shark knows its position with respect to the downward pull of gravity, and its orientation and direction of movement.

thunder to the higher notes of the human voice. Lower frequencies have more effect, especially when they are irregular—as generated by an injured, thrashing animal. These pressure waves can be detected more than 650 feet away.

The ears may also be important in general navigation (see page 104).

SENSE AND SUPERSENSE

Touch at a Distance

right: **The lateral line of the leopard shark shows as a lengthwise raised stripe along the side of the body.**

far right: **The lateral line senses movements and pressure changes in the water. This nurse shark may be able to feel ripples breaking on the nearby beach.**

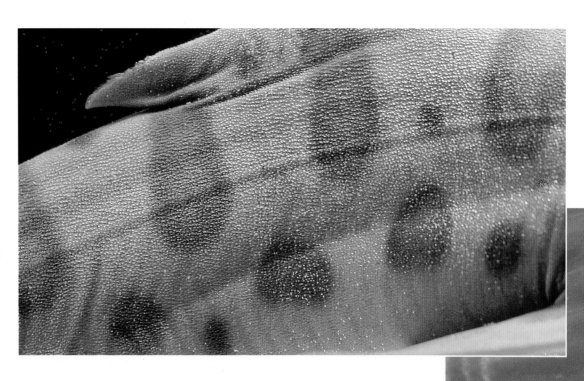

The lateral line system consists of a tiny tunnel-like canal just under the skin on each side of the shark, connected to the outside by numerous tiny tubes that open at holes in the shark's skin.

The canal is lined with hundreds of neuromasts, which are bunches of mechanoreceptor sensory hair cells (see page 98). For each bunch, their microhair tips are embedded in a jelly lump, the cupola, or simply project into the water in the canal. As the shark swims, the water swishes past its skin and sets up currents in the water within the lateral line canal. These currents push and sway the cupolas and hairs in a certain way, which stimulates the nerve cells to send signals to the brain.

patterns of information

The lateral line system also reacts to variations in water currents around the shark, and pressure waves from underwater sounds. Every second it sends millions of nerve signals, from the thousands of clusters of sensory hair cells inside the canals, to the brain. So the shark is exceptionally aware of its surroundings and has plenty of information about ripples, eddies, movements, and vibrations in the water around it.

As a current flows around a nearby projecting rock, or a passing fish swishes its tail, this also affects the pattern of water movements, and the pattern of nerve signals from the lateral line system to the brain alters as a result. The lateral line is probably also important in general navigation (see page 104).

Perhaps the nearest sensation that we as humans get to the lateral line of the shark, is feeling the wind on our faces and skin when we are outside, and then not feeling it when we walk indoors.

SENSE AND SUPERSENSE

a touchy subject

Our skin can feel light touch, heavier pressure, small variations in heat and cold, and surfaces that are rough or smooth, dry or moist, hard or soft. Sharks probably do not have such a detailed sense of touch. They do not really need it—they have their lateral lines, and they make physical contact with few animals and objects.

Their skin can detect a certain amount of basic contact, larger-scale changes in temperature, noxious or corrosive chemicals in the water, and physical damage. These are detected by the bare endings of sensory nerves, called free nerve endings, embedded in the skin.

THE INNER SENSE

Like other animals, sharks need information about their internal body organs and processes. This ranges from knowing when to stop eating because the stomach is full to bursting, or when urine must be expelled, to whether the muscles are pulling the tail to the left or right, for a smooth, coordinated swimming motion. Microscopic sensory cells called proprioceptors are scattered throughout the muscles, joints, digestive system, blood vessels, and other inner body parts. They can detect when these parts are being bent, stretched, or squashed. This is the shark's sense of position, posture, and internal functioning, called the proprioceptive sense.

Sixth Senses

ANY MUSCLE ACTIVITY OF A LIVING CREATURE CREATES FIELDS OF ELECTRICITY. (WE DETECT THESE PULSES FROM OUR OWN HEARTS AND CAN SEE THEM AS AN ELECTROCARDIAGRAM TRACE.)

For animals on land, electricity cannot travel away from their bodies, since air is a very poor electrical conductor. But water is a very good electrical conductor.

Several groups of animals, including sharks and rays, can detect the tiny electrical pulses in the water around them from the muscle movements of other creatures. This electrical sense helps them to navigate and detect prey. Even a prey creature that keeps still, hiding in weeds or mud, gives off these electrical pulses, since its breathing and heart muscles are always active.

electricity sensors

The shark's electricity-sensing devices are clusters of tiny pores or cavities in the skin around its head and front end. They are called ampullae of Lorenzini. Actively hunting sharks have 1,500 or more ampullae. Sluggish bottom-dwellers have only a few hundred.

Each ampulla consists of a pore in the skin's surface, leading into an almost microscopic bottle-shaped pit filled with jelly. The pit walls are lined with sensory cells that resemble the sensory hair cells in the ears and lateral lines. But these ampulla cells lack hairs. They are adapted to send nerve signals to the brain when they are stimulated by electrical pulses through the water. They also react, to a lesser degree, to changes in water pressure and temperature.

In experiments, if a shark's senses are temporarily blocked with layers of jelly, apart from the ampullae, it can still find a flatfish buried in sand or mud. But it cannot find a flatfish which is electrically insulated with a special wire mesh that takes away the electrical pulses.

a detailed sense

The ampullae are remarkably sensitive. They can detect a change in voltage with distance, called a voltage gradient, of just 10 millionths of a volt per centimeter (or half-inch). This would be equivalent to attaching two wires to a single 1.5-volt AA-type battery and dipping the ends of the wires into the sea water—1.5 kilometers (or nearly a mile) apart. Such sensitivity is easily sufficient to detect the electrical pulses given off by another animal's muscle activity. The

above: **A mormyrid or elephant-snout fish probes with its electrically sensitive snout.**

DETECTING THE DETECTORS

The electricity-detecting skin ampullae scattered over a shark's head were first discovered by the famous Italian microscopist, Marcello Malpighi, in 1663. (Malpighi also made many discoveries about human anatomy, such as kidney renal tubules, and blood capillaries.) The ampullae were first described in detail by Stefano Lorenzini in 1678, which is why they bear his name. It was not until almost 300 years later, in the 1960s, that their function was understood.

The head shapes of some sharks may have evolved to increase their sensitivity even further. A hammerhead shark uses its flattened "hammer" head like a metal detector, sweeping it to and fro over the sea bed, to detect electrical signals from buried prey. Its nostrils are also farther apart than normal, for improved sensing of the direction of a scent (see page 94). The strange deep-sea goblin shark probably uses its shovel-nose in a similar fashion.

tricking the senses

A shark may attack a metal electrode (rod) dipped into the water, which is emitting electrical pulses. Presumably it mistakes this for a prey animal. In fact, the shark may prefer biting the electrode to attacking a real prey animal. It seems that electricity detection is the main sense, rather than sight or hearing, when a shark is close to prey.

Most metals corrode in salty sea water, and this produces electricity. (Metals in salt solutions work like a type of battery.) This is probably why sharks sometimes attack the metal safety cages containing human observers and photographers. The salts and minerals in the leaking body fluids of an injured animal or person also create a certain type of electrical signal, which may explain why sharks keep attacking the original victim and ignore uninjured rescuers.

above: **A shark's electro-receptors are scattered in tiny pits over the skin of its snout and head.**

left top: **An electric catfish senses electrical ripples in the water.**

breathing movements and heartbeat of a resting flatfish like a plaice give off voltages 100,000 times stronger. In fact, the shark is so amazingly sensitive that it could detect the minute voltages produced by the nerve signals inside an animal's body. We detect nerve signals in our own brains using the EEG, electroencephalograph. So the shark is a type of living EEG machine.

TO US, THE OPEN OCEAN IS FEATURELESS. WE HAVE NO LANDMARKS OR ANY CLUES TO OUR LOCATION, UNLESS WE ARE TRAINED IN NAVIGATION USING A MAGNETIC COMPASS, AND THE POSITIONS OF THE SUN, MOON, AND STARS.

above: **Sharks, like this sand tiger, are probably capable of sensing and analyzing all manner of stimuli in what we would regard as perfectly uniform sea water.**

How do sharks accurately find their way around? They, unlike us, realize that the oceans are far from uniform.

One type of variation is in the water itself—in its speed, strength, and direction of movement, and its physical and chemical make-up. There are relatively permanent "landmarks" in the oceans where streams or currents of water cross each other, or flow over underwater cliffs and along deep-sea valleys. The currents contain water at different temperatures, densities, chemical concentrations, and pressures. They flow horizontally, vertically, and diagonally.

Sharks are highly tuned to this world of scents, chemicals, salt concentrations, temperatures, and pressures. They can use the currents as guides when navigating.

clues from sounds

Sounds in the sea are another important clue to location and direction. Scientists are only just beginning to understand that the oceans are full of background noise from turbulent water, animals, boats, and other sources. (It's similar to the background hubbub of vehicles, machines, planes, trains, and people in a city.) Recent research shows that this background of "wet noise" may form a type of detailed sound image, showing the shark its position. The lateral line system and ears would help the shark to form sound pictures of its surroundings. Scientists use similar passive sonar, or sound-detecting, systems called sonograms to map the sea bed and objects in the water.

Water's temperature, density, and flow affect the speed and distance that sounds travel through it. So the physical and chemical make-up of sea water interacts with its sound-carrying or acoustic properties. There are doubtless other interactions, including electricity and magnetism, waiting for our discovery.

a magnetic sense?

Many experts believe that sharks use their electricity-detecting sense as their main aid to navigation on long migrations. The laws of physics tell us that when electrically charged particles move through a magnetic field, they generate electricity. It is possible that when salty sea water, full of dissolved and electrically charged particles called salt ions, moves through the Earth's own natural magnetic field, this generates weak patterns of electricity. Sharks may sense these, and the way they vary with the direction of water flow and its orientation to the Earth's north–south lines of magnetic force. The electrical patterns may provide "route signs" for the shark's journey.We are only just beginning to understand the complexity of the so-called "featureless" open ocean—something that sharks have known for millions of years (see pages 106—107).

right: **Some termites were thought to detect Earth's magnetism because their slab-like nest mounds are orientated North-South. But the reason is probably temperature regulation, to avoid the fierce midday sun shining on the wider side and overheating the nest.**

THE BUILT-IN COMPASS?

A shark is itself full of dissolved and electrically charged particles, ions, in its body salts, minerals, fluids, and tissues. So, as the shark swims through the Earth's weak magnetic field, it may generate its own patterns of electricity. It's possible that the shark can sense these with its electricity-detecting ampullae. The strength and direction of the electrical voltage produced would vary according to the shark's orientation to the Earth's magnetic field. In effect, this would give the shark a built-in electromagnetic compass. However, our research into this aspect of shark senses is merely beginning.

Finding their Way: 2

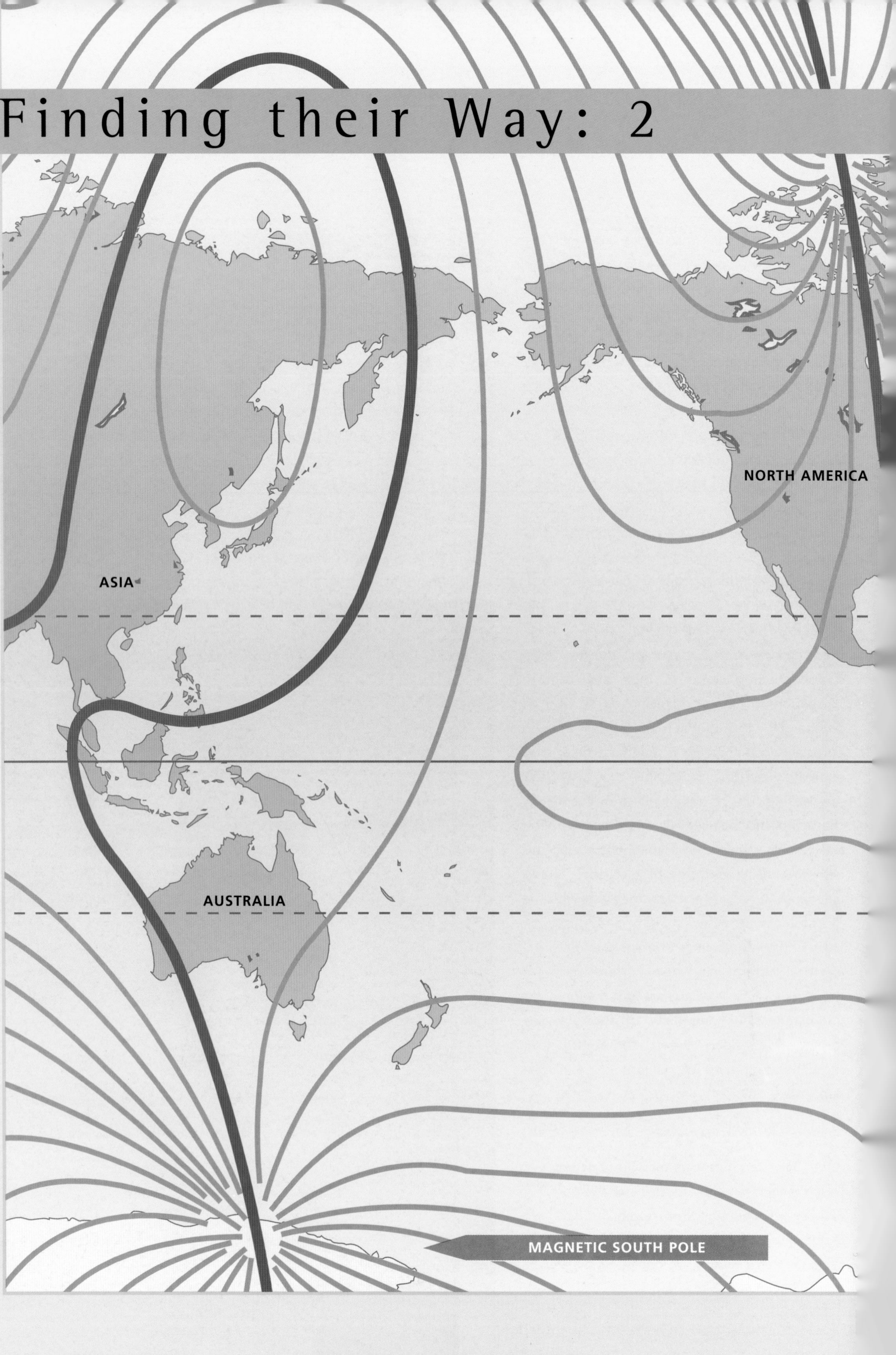

NORTH AMERICA

ASIA

AUSTRALIA

MAGNETIC SOUTH POLE

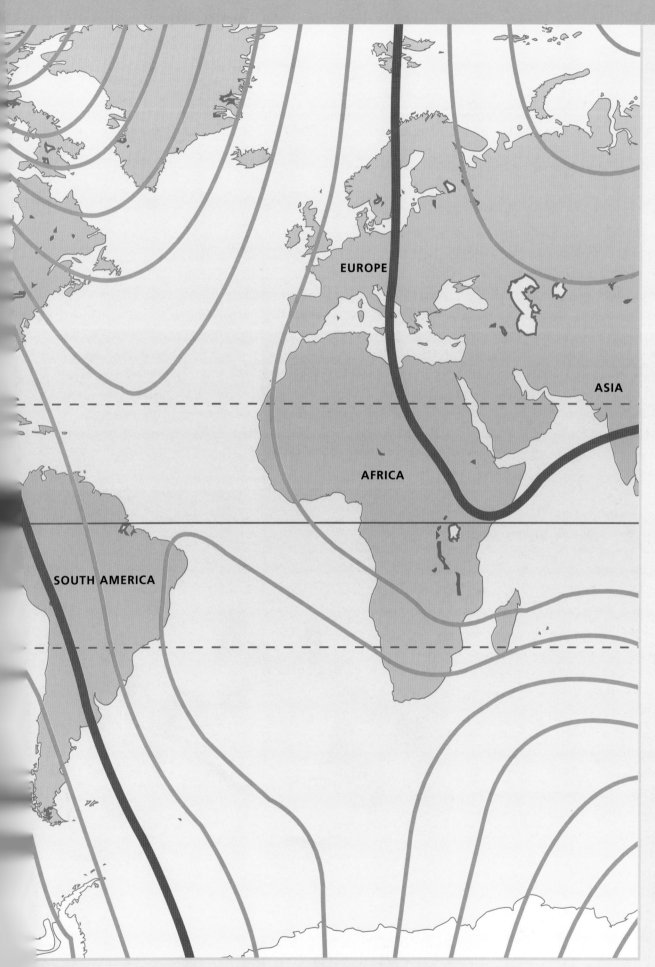

EUROPE

ASIA

AFRICA

SOUTH AMERICA

left: The earth is a giant magnet and has a magnetic field, which our compass needles detect. However, because of the composition of rocks, the field is not constant. The contours on this world map show where magnetic variations occur.

SENSE AND SUPERSENSE

Bright Sharks?

IN TERMS OF EVOLUTION, SHARKS HAVE RELATIVELY PRIMITIVE AND SIMPLE BRAINS, COMPARED WITH, FOR EXAMPLE, BIRDS AND MAMMALS (SEE PAGE 92). ALSO, DETAILS OF SHARK BEHAVIOR ARE DIFFICULT TO STUDY IN THE WILD.

So sharks have long been thought to function like unthinking robotic eating machines with almost no intelligence. But recent studies show that this is far from the case.

However simple the shark brain may appear to be, it has served the shark extremely well for hundreds of millions of years. So it may be ancient, primitive, and unsophisticated, but it certainly cannot be regarded as inferior to the brains of other vertebrates, in terms of evolutionary success.

Experiments and observations of both wild and captive sharks are slowly dispelling the myth of the shark as an unthinking, unintelligent robot. Studies are revealing that these creatures remember, learn from experience, communicate, and interact with others of their own kind, and with other animals in the sea.

instinct and learning

Certain types of behavior are based on in-built patterns. These are called instinctive responses. They usually happen in reaction to certain specific stimulations. These instincts are a result of genetic instructions inherited from ancestors. Just like body shape or tooth size, instinctive behavior is coded into the genes, and subject to the forces of evolution.

In many animals, instinctive responses can be modified to some degree, by decisions based on experience. The animal confronts a situation, behaves in a certain way, assesses the results of this behavior and forms a memory. Next time it meets the same situation, it recalls its previous experience, and perhaps modifies or changes its behavior, in a trial-and-error fashion. This is the basis of simple learning.

The next stage in sophistication is to learn by thought and reasoning in the brain alone, without the body having to go through the situation in real life at all. This power of abstract thought and reason, involving anticipation and planning, is where humans exceed all other creatures.

simple, but not stupid

It was once thought that animals near the "lower" end of the evolutionary scale, who had appeared early in the evolutionary process, behaved mainly by unmodified instinctive

below: **A graytip reef shark has learned that a diver-type shape means potential food. The diver has also learned—how to feed the shark.**

responses. They had little capacity for learning. The behavior of "higher" vertebrates, on the other hand, such as mammals, resulted mainly from learning. Many scientists now think that this is an oversimplification.

Experiments with sharks have shown that they are as capable of learning and modifying their behavior as small mammals such as mice and shrews. In aquaria, sharks can learn to take food from their trainer. They can also discriminate by sight between shapes and learn, for example, that a circle signifies food but a square does not.

In the wild, sharks learn by themselves to harass spear-fishing humans, who avoid attack by giving up their catches. Some sharks learn where and when to wait for abundant seasonal prey, such as young sea birds or seals. There are more examples on the following pages.

top: **Friends? For now, perhaps, in the limited way that big cats such as lions are "tame". Natural instincts could erupt any second.**

above: **The dolphin's brain is far bigger and more sophisticated than any shark's. But the difference in intelligence could be more in degree, rather than absolute type.**

Getting On With Others

AS WE'VE SEEN, SHARKS HAVE EXPRESSIONLESS FACES AND FAIRLY RIGID BODIES. SO ANY

MOVEMENTS AND POSTURES THEY MAY MAKE, TO INDICATE THEIR MOODS AND INTENTIONS,

ARE SUBTLE AND DIFFICULT FOR HUMANS TO INTERPRET.

above: **This gray reef shark has adopted an aggressive-type posture, with its body arched downwards, its snout cocked up, and its pectoral (front side) fins lowered to form an upside-down V. This compares to ...**

Experienced divers have come to recognize and understand sharks' behavior when they're "threatened" by human divers in their midst. Gray reef, silky, and similar sharks typically respond to the intruder by swimming in erratic figures-of-eight with back arched, snout raised and pectoral (front side) fins dipped. The great white shark may gape its mouth to show its teeth, and perhaps slap its tail in the direction of the intruder. When it hunches its body and dips its pectoral fins, this reveals a dark spot—perhaps a warning sign.

Such actions can be interpreted as self-defense on the part of the shark. But they may easily tip into aggression. They are ignored at the diver's peril.

reacting to events

An Australian marine biologist, Jim MacKay, carried out some potentially dangerous behavior studies on sharks such as great whites, tigers, and makos. While diving with them, he trained them to take bait fish from the end of his spear. Then he recorded the responses of the sharks to his own behavior while he fed them like this.

If he remained calm and confident, with smooth and coordinated movements, dominant and in control, the sharks did not become threatening at all. But if he feigned panic, with jerky actions and submissive gestures, the sharks became more excited and aggressive. They were analyzing his own behavior, and reacting accordingly.

Most sharks have no obvious means of making sounds for communication, other than by thrashing the water. Whale sharks have been heard emitting low croaking grunts. Wobbegongs are reputed to utter "gruff-chuff" as they adjust their mouthgrip on prey. Swell sharks have been heard to "bark." But the purpose of these sounds is unknown.

do sharks play?

Sharks have demonstrated behavior that is not directly concerned with feeding or survival. In other animals, like dolphins and otters in water, or cats and monkeys on land, it might be described as curiosity, even play.

Great white sharks are notoriously curious. They approach, nudge, and even gently mouth objects that they find floating at the surface. Their aim may be to investigate the object's food potential. But even well-fed sharks do this. Perhaps they are logging the experience into the memory, for future reference.

Penguins are not a normal part of a shark's diet. But some species of sharks grab these aquatic birds, and throw them about on the ocean surface like toys. After a time the shark usually loses interest, and swims off without consuming this potential snack. Amazingly, the penguins often survive this traumatic event, though perhaps a little worse for wear. The struggles, sound, scent, or taste of the penguin cannot be very significant, since great white sharks do the same to wooden model penguins. Observers suggest that the sharks are practicing their hunting and catching techniques. In a kitten pouncing on a toy mouse, this would be called "play."

Porbeagle sharks are often seen in loose groups of 20 or so, similarly manipulating and flicking floating objects such as lumber or seaweed.

above: ... **the normal swimming attitude with a straighter body, level snout, and more horizontal pectoral fins. Such differences seem subtle to us, but not if our lives depend on interpreting them.**

SENSE AND SUPERSENSE

Are Sharks Social?

SHARKS MAY WELL COMMUNICATE WITH OTHERS OF THEIR KIND IN VARIOUS WAYS,
USING THEIR COMPLEX SENSES—ESPECIALLY BY SCENT SUBSTANCES CALLED PHEROMONES,
WHICH THEY RELEASE INTO THE WATER TO SIGNAL THEIR INTENTIONS, SUCH AS
READINESS TO MATE OR ATTACK.

right: **Whitetip reef sharks gather in a shelter under rocks for a communal rest.**

opposite page: **Blacktip reef sharks cruise in numbers, on the lookout for prey. Most such gatherings are at particularly rich feeding grounds, in the way that normally solitary vultures congregate at a carcass.**

However, since we do not fully understand the shark's sensory powers, researchers have plenty to do on this aspect of their lives.

safety in numbers

Some sharks gather in large single-species groups, called shoals or schools, but their reasons are not yet clear. The groups probably provide protection for their members, since predators are less likely to attack such a massed gathering. However, most of the larger sharks have very few enemies—apart from other, larger, sharks.

Whitetip reef sharks and tiger sharks rest by day in large groups in caves or under rock overhangs. With their collective awareness, using many pairs of eyes, lateral lines and other senses, they may be able to detect danger or prey more effectively. On the other hand, they may simply congregate at the site because it's the most suitable resting place.

When nurse sharks rest on the bottom, they may lie one on another, like puppies in a heap. Tactile (touch) communication may play a part in these gatherings, relating to courtship or dominance (see panel).

finding mates

A second possible reason for schooling behavior is to increase reproductive success. Compared with a solitary life, gathering in groups allows individuals to be more aware of the maturity and sexual condition of potential mates, and it provides opportunities for breeding. However, some species, like spurdogs and lemon sharks, live in single-sex schools outside the breeding season. Mating cannot be their aim.

Scalloped hammerhead sharks are nocturnal hunters. By day they rest, swimming lazily in schools of many hundreds. They move and turn in coordinated fashion, like other shoals of fish. But the females, who may outnumber the males by four to one, jostle and head-butt each other to stay in the center. They may have a better chance of mating here, although it has never been observed. The daytime hammerhead schools may just be safe refuges.

hunting together

A third reason for shoaling could be to hunt as a pack, and increase food-catching success. Many sharks feed in large groups (see page 158). They

may merely gather at the site because food is abundant, and have no interactions with their fellow species members.

Intriguingly, observations of great white sharks suggest that they cooperate while hunting. Each individual responds to the movements of others in its group. The shoal members develop interactive relationships and behavior patterns. For example, two individuals may form a close partnership, feeding at each other's catches as though "sharing" food, and even traveling together during many years to seasonal feeding grounds.

WHO'S BOSS IN THE SHARK SHOAL?

In many single-species groups of animals, from lions to crocodiles, there is a dominance hierarchy. The group has its chiefs or bosses. They get first choice of food, rest sites, and mates, while others are submissive to them. They maintain their position by displays of health and strength, threats, and—rarely—physical combat. From its recognition in flocks of farmyard chickens, this is called the "pecking order." Sharks in large groups have been seen to head-butt each other with open jaws, their teeth leaving minor wounds in the opponent. These actions do not seem to be full attacks. Perhaps they are ways of settling dominance disputes within the shoal. In general terms, large sharks tend to be dominant over smaller sharks.

SENSE AND SUPERSENSE

113

CHAPTER 5

Design For Living

The Survival Suite

All parts of the shark's body—its overall shape, the fins and tail, skin and teeth, and the muscles and skeleton within—contribute to the superb shark design.

Within the general shark shape, there are many variations. Some kinds are supremely streamlined swimming machines. They can cut through the water with the merest flick of the tail, and outpace most of their supposedly more "advanced" cousins, the bony fish. Their fins and tails are surfaces for propulsion and maneuvering, shaped and placed for maximum efficiency and control, while minimizing wasted energy in the form of eddies and currents in the water, as they slip past. Other sharks lurk near or on the bottom, supple and maneuverable, ready for ambush action. Whatever their place or niche in nature, they are equipped with components of the highest quality.

outside in

On the outside of the shark is its skin. Crucial to life, it provides protection like a tough armor of prickly chain mail, to deter would-be attackers. It is an all-over covering that holds the whole creature together; it creates color and texture and camouflage; and it provides a slippery, low-drag surface when moving. It can even provide floppy flaps, frilly trimmings, or illuminated lures, to enhance deception. The skin contains or supports highly tuned sensor organs, and permits a carefully controlled exchange of water, salts, minerals, and other substances, between sea water outside and body fluids and tissues within.

previous page: **The wobbegong's skin helps to camouflage it as it lies in reefs or on the seabed.**

Under the skin is an exquisite system of dozens of muscles, honed by evolution to generate maximum power and control, with minimum bulk and energy consumption. Their directions of contraction and lines of pull could not be bettered by the most up-to-date computer-aided design system. The muscles are anchored to the gristly or cartilaginous skeleton, light yet tough, which gives the shark extraordinary tensile strength with relative flexibility.

below: **From the sandy seabed of Jervis Bay, NSW, Australia, an angelshark rears up and snaps.**

left: **Who's hiding here? The eyes of a shovelnose shark or ray peer from the ocean-bottom sediment, watching for prey or danger.**

Shark Shapes

above: **The unmistakable sleek, speedy, streamlined profile of a typical shark—in this case, a blue shark near the coast of California.**

The shark's body is basically torpedo-shaped, or fusiform, with a wider and taller middle, and tapering ends. Most sharks have two back or dorsal fins which stick up from the upper surface, and two pairs of fins that project at an angle, out and downward from the underside. These are the pectoral fins in front and the pelvic fins behind. There is usually also a smaller, single anal fin at the rear of the underside, and the large caudal fin—better known as the tail.

The front end of a fast-swimming shark, like the mako or blue shark, has a pointed wedge shape. This offers minimal resistance to the water, while still housing the eyes and other sense organs, and an effective mouth. The head may be flattened slightly to act as a hydrofoil and counteract the shark's natural tendency to sink (see page 124).

The rear of the shark's body narrows to the tail stem or peduncle, to reduce the resistance set up by moving through water (see page 122). It is also flattened from side to side, to increase the effectiveness of the tail's propulsive swimming movements. There are sometimes ridges or keels along the peduncle, like tiny vertical fins, as on the whale shark or porbeagle. These help to stabilize the body and stop it rolling from side to side.

flat bottoms

Sharks that live on the sea bed, like carpet and angelsharks, have little need of swift movement

COPYCAT DESIGNS

Human designers and engineers have come up with the same basic shape for moving through the water, as sharks and similar sea creatures who have undergone parallel or convergent evolution (see page 37). Submarines, boat hulls, and torpedoes have a similar outline to the standard shark, with a wide middle that tapers at both ends. This maximizes energy use and minimizes drag.

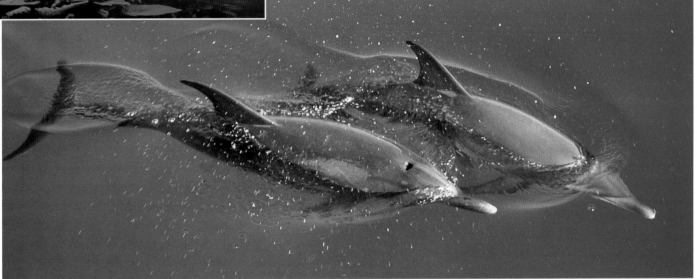

and streamlining. So they resemble a "normal" shark that has been run over by a steamroller.

Their lifestyles depend on not being seen, and they rely more on camouflage and concealment than on speed. The head and body is wide and flat, with large and rounded fins attached to the sides, rather than to the underside. The dorsal fins are small and near the rear, toward the tail. The anal fin is also small, as is the caudal fin or tail, since powerful tail-flicks are little used.

shapes and sizes

There are many other shapes of sharks between the two extremes of fast swimmer and flat-bottomed, sea-bed dweller. Species that live near rather than on the bottom, like dogfish, are more snakelike. They wriggle among the weeds with long, narrow, eel-like bodies, wide and rounded pairs of side fins, and small back fins. Their heads are large and blunt-snouted.

Sharks that live in very deep water, like the megamouth and sleeper, tend to have rounded, flabby, floppy bodies. This is an adaptation to the immense pressures in the depths. The surrounding water does the job of pressing on, supporting, and containing the body. So the skin functions not as a restraining container, but more as a loose bag for holding the contents. These species swim slowly, and so need little streamlining, and they do not rest on the sea bed, so they need no flatness.

top left: **Ocean-going bony fish, like this yellowfin tuna, have a similar overall shape, but with a body more flattened side to side, flexible fins, and symmetrical tail.**

above: **As the dolphin's dorsal fin breaks the surface, it is seen as more crescentic, rather than triangular like the typical shark's.**

Moving Through Water

THE EASE AND GRACE OF A SHARK BELIES THE DIFFICULTY OF MOVING THROUGH WATER. ANYONE WHO WALKS IN WATER OR SWIMS REGULARLY KNOWS THE HARD WORK REQUIRED TO PUSH THROUGH THIS RELATIVELY DENSE MEDIUM AND OVERCOME THE LIQUID'S RESISTANCE.

right: **This blacktip reef shark displays its upward-tilted, wedge-shaped snout, which helps to provide lift as the fish powers forward.**

opposite: **The leopard shark's tail finishes its swish to the right, as the S-shaped swimming curve "throws off" its end. Note the sharksucker fish under its right front side.**

below: **This diagram of a swimming dogfish shows how S-shaped curves pass along its body, increasing in size as they reach the tail.**

Water is viscous, thick, and glutinous. It is more than 1,000 times heavier or denser than an equal volume of our own medium, the air of the Earth's atmosphere. Water strongly opposes being pushed aside or out of the way, producing a force against motion, called resistance. And it clings or adheres to anything trying to move through it, holding on like glue, with a force called drag. Another problem is that in mid-water, there is no fixed surface or anchorage point to push against while moving; on land, we have the ground.

The shark has not only overcome these problems, but uses them to advantage. The streamlined shape is designed to minimize both resistance and drag. Imagine a cone pulled through the water. Blunt end first, it offers maximum resistance, but little drag as the water slides off the tapering point. Pointed end first, it offers little resistance but maximum drag. Stick the blunt ends of two cones together, and the resulting sharklike shape offers least resistance and least drag.

thrust for propulsion

The way to overcome both resistance and drag, and move along, is by a forward force—thrust. This comes from the shark's swishing body and tail. It works according to Isaac Newton's third law of motion. This states that, when a force on a body causes an action, it is opposed by an equal and opposite reaction.

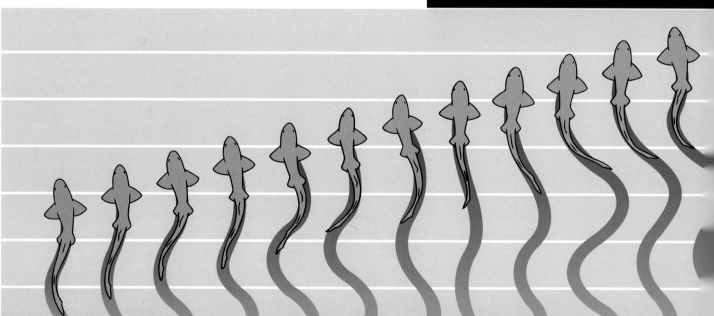

As a shark swims, its body undulates from side to side with S-like curves. This presses on the water around, which pushes back with equal and opposite force. The sideways motions cancel each other out. The rearward force pushes the water back, and the water resists by forcing the shark forward. The curviness or amplitude of each wave gets larger as it passes along the shark's body, from head to tail. This has the effect of increasing the push on the water. The final thrust is given by the tail or caudal fin, which traces a spiral figure-of-eight through the water—just as an oarsman with a single rear paddle gyrates it in figure-8s to propel the boat.

Any object moving through water generates eddies, vortices, and turbulence. Sharks use the turbulence they set up to overcome the lack of firm anchorage points when moving (see pages 122 and 132).

ALMOST WEIGHTLESS

One advantage of living in water is that it provides support and buoyancy. Its density buffers the effects of gravity. Sharks and other water dwellers do not have to use as much energy as land animals, who need to stay upright and overcome gravity as they run and leap. Also, a shark that swims near to the surface builds up energy by virtue of its movement (kinetic energy of motion) and relatively high level (potential energy of position). It may even use warm, rising ocean currents to achieve greater height above the sea bed. Like a bird that soars high and glides back to Earth, the shark can use this energy to swim or drift onward, almost effortlessly.

Tails and Fins

IN BONY FISH, THE CAUDAL FIN OR TAIL IS USED FOR PROPULSION, AND THE VARIOUS BODY FINS ARE FOR MANEUVERING AND CONTROL.

The fins can be fanned out, folded up, bent and tilted at different angles to the body. The fish can use them as auxiliary rudders to turn left or right, as hydrofoils (the watery version of a plane's elevators) to go up and down, and as brakes to stop suddenly.

But most sharks do not have this flexibility. Their fins are different in structure. They lack a bony fish's fin rays, or the delicate muscles which move them, or the thin, elastic fin membrane. A shark's vertical fins—dorsal, anal, and caudal— are relatively stiff and rigid, fixed in shape and angle. This places limitations on the shark's maneuverability and fine control when moving through the water.

the tail

The rear end of the shark's spinal or vertebral column bears the two-lobed caudal fin, which is supported by cartilaginous rods within, and by dermal (skin) filaments. The spinal column projects into the upper lobe of the tail. This is called the heterocercal design. It differs radically from most bony fish, in which the spinal column ends before the tail starts, and the two tail lobes are equal—called the homocercal design.

In some sharks the spinal column has a kink and turns upward into the tail's upper lobe. In others it is straight, and the tail is kinked down slightly to fit on to it. Great white sharks, makos, and porbeagles have a tail whose upper and lower lobes are outwardly almost symmetrical, like the homocercal tails of most bony fish, but the inner structure is still heterocercal.

dorsal fins

The dorsal fins of sharks are permanently erect. They cannot be folded flat against the back, to reduce drag, like the fins of swordfish, tuna, and similar speedy bony fish. But sharks use the

LONG-TAILED SHARKS

Thresher sharks appear to have an extreme version of the heterocercal tail. The upper lobe is much longer than the lower one—even longer than the rest of the body. But the thresher does not constantly dive downward, as would be expected (see page 124). This is because the long upper tail lobe is aligned with the body, as a direct rearward extension of it. The small lower lobe projects below.

Threshers have many other descriptive names, such as fox sharks, swingletails, swiveltails, or simply long-tailed sharks.

right: **The diagrams show the fins of a whitetip shark. These fish combine fast bursts of speed with delicate maneuvering as they search for victims among the coral crevices.**

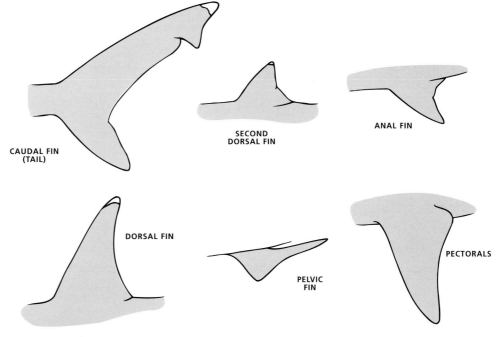

CAUDAL FIN
(TAIL)

SECOND
DORSAL FIN

ANAL FIN

DORSAL FIN

PELVIC
FIN

PECTORALS

below: **In the Coral Sea, a silvertip shark demonstrates its complement of fins and the typical shark heterocercal tail, with its larger upper lobe.**

turbulence created by the dorsal fins as pivot points, to help push themselves through the water. The two dorsal fins, and probably the tail too, are spaced in such a way that the swirling eddy or vortex created by the first fin is in just the right place, as the shark moves forward and its body undulates, for the second fin to push against, as it arrives there. On the next undulation down the body, as the shark continues forward, the tail arrives at the same place, and again makes use of the vortex. On land, a similar process might be stepping in someone else's footprints on the wet sand of a beach, since the sand there is already compressed, and this gives a firmer base for the foot to push off.

side fins

The pectoral and pelvic fins of most sharks are tilted slightly, with the front or leading edge aiming up. This tends to lift the front end of the shark as it swims forward, like the hydrofoils on a submarine, to counteract the sinking effects of the heavy body and the heterocercal tail.

Most sharks can adjust the angles of these fins to an extent, to control rising and descending (see page 136).

Bottom-living epaulette and horn sharks have developed another use for their side fins. They "crawl" on them, along the sea bed.

D E S I G N   F O R   L I V I N G

Sink or Swim

IT WAS ONCE THOUGHT THAT SHARKS NEEDED TO SWIM CONSTANTLY TO STAY ALIVE. IN FACT THEY MUST SWIM CONSTANTLY TO STAY OFF THE BOTTOM—BUT NOT ALL SHARKS NEED TO STAY OFF THE BOTTOM.

A shark's body tissues are denser and heavier than water, so the natural tendency is for a shark to sink slowly. To counteract this inconvenience, it has various buoyancy aids. One is the cartilaginous skeleton, which is lighter than the equivalent bone version. Another is a large, oily liver, which may take up as much as one-fifth of the body volume. It contains a fatty substance called squalene (see page 17). Like most oils, this is lighter than water. Squalene has a density of 0·86, compared with sea water at 1·026, and the rest of the shark's body at about 1·1. So the liver helps to keep the shark afloat. Whale and basking sharks have particularly huge livers, to help them maintain their optimum feeding position near the water's surface.

no swim bladder

Bony fish control buoyancy using a swim bladder. It is a saclike extension of the gut. Bubbles of gases can be introduced into it from the blood, or withdrawn from it. More bubbles make the whole fish lighter and less dense, and so it rises through the water. The fish's control must be precise, since depth and water pressure affect the bubbles. With exactly the right buoyancy, the bony fish can swim level and even "hang" in mid-water.

Sharks do not have a true swim bladder. It was one of the chance vagaries of evolution. Not to be outdone, however, a few types can use gas to help them maintain buoyancy, by gulping air into the gut. Captive sandsharks have been seen doing this at the surface of their tank. They then hold their position in the water, motionless and without effort, for some time.

COUNTERACTING THE DIVE

A problem with a shark's heterocercal or unequal tail lobes, with the upper one larger than the lower, extending above the body line, is that swishing the tail tends to drive the nose down. This is counteracted by the side fins, which are angled upward like hydrofoils, as we saw on page 123. The wedge-shaped snout also has the same effect, forcing the nose up. This is taken to extremes in the hammerhead, with its wide, hydrofoil-type head.

But this system works only while the shark moves at speed. When an airplane's engines stop, it falls to the ground. Likewise, when a shark stops swimming, it tends to sink to the bottom.

LIVER

SHARK

CUTTLEFISH

CUTTLEBONE

BONY FISH

SWIM BLADDER

above: **The buoyancy devices of three marine creatures: the oil-filled liver of a shark (top); the low-density cuttlebone of a cuttlefish (left); and the gas-filled swimbladder of a bony fish.**

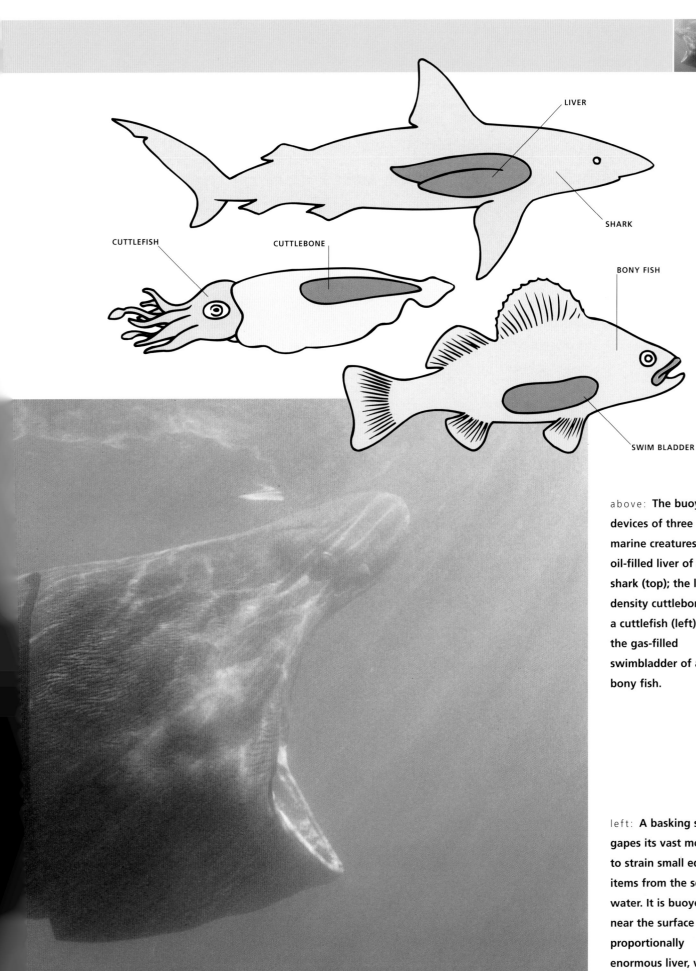

left: **A basking shark gapes its vast mouth to strain small edible items from the sea water. It is buoyed up near the surface by its proportionally enormous liver, which is rich in lighter-than-water oils.**

125

MOST SHARKS HUNT BY STEALTH. THE COLORS AND PATTERNS ON THEIR BODIES ARE MAINLY FOR CAMOUFLAGE AND DISGUISE. BUT VISION IS MORE BLURRED AND LIMITED IN THE DIM UNDERWATER WORLD.

Also, sea water absorbs some colors of the light spectrum more than others, dulling reds and yellows, especially. So shark coloration may not seem incredibly effective to our own eyes. But it must work for the shark.

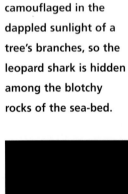

below: **As a leopard is camouflaged in the dappled sunlight of a tree's branches, so the leopard shark is hidden among the blotchy rocks of the sea-bed.**

Coloring substances, or pigments, are produced in the shark's skin by microscopic star-shaped cells: chromatophores. The molecules of pigment can be moved within each cell. If they are all condensed into the cell's center, the color of the tissues behind shows through, and the shark's skin appears light. If the pigment molecules are spread out in their cell, the skin takes on their color—usually dark.

changing colors

Most sharks develop and keep the same colors through life. In some species, the young start life in the shallows, and have beautiful markings to camouflage and protect them there, until they grow large enough to venture into deeper water, when they become duller. For example, the leopard shark starts life with the spots of its big-cat namesake, but loses them as it gets older. Likewise the zebra shark has stripes when young, but these change with age, to spots.

Some horn sharks wear dramatic zebra-like stripes or giraffe-like blotches in the early years, but these fade with age. The sand tiger lives in

above: **The blue-gray bodies of these bull sharks merge into the cloudy, muddy, shadowless waters of bays and estuaries.**

top: **The blue shark has the countershading typical of open-ocean surface-dwellers, with darker topside and lighter underside.**

NAMED FROM THEIR COLORS

• The skaamoog or shy-eye has beautiful markings that have been described as resembling the hieroglyphs of ancient Egypt.

• The chain dogfish, *Scyliorhinus retifer*, seems to have large chains wrapped around its body.

• The marbled dogfish, *Atelomycterus marmoratus*, and the marbled catshark, *Galeus arae* resemble the swirling patterns in marble rock.

sandy shallows all its life. Despite its stripe-suggesting name, it has golden spots for disguise.

Sharks must see their surroundings, since when they have a choice, they select patches of sea bed that suit their camouflage. The lesser spotted or sandy dogfish, *Scyliorhinus caniculus*, has dark yellowish-gray spots and prefers the sandy sea bed. The greater spotted dogfish, *Scyliorhinus stellaris*, on the other hand, has reddish spots and selects a more pebbly bottom.

A few sharks, like the wobbegong, can change their skin color slowly, over several hours or days. But this is slow compared with the second-by-second flashes of hue and pattern shown by other marine creatures, especially cuttlefish and squid.

Many sharks of open water have darker backs and lighter undersides. This is called countershading and it is common among surface-dwelling fish of all kinds, from tuna and marlin to mackerel and herring. It counteracts the effect of sunlight from above (see page 68).

Vision is very poor in cloudy water. So sharks that lurk in murky, muddy offshore areas, like nurse and bull sharks, are generally blue-gray. In the sea's depths there is no light at all. Sharks who dwell here, such as the megamouth and the lantern shark, are all-over dark or black.

Cunning Disguises

A FEW SHARKS HAVE EXTRA TRICKS OF DISGUISE, APART FROM BASIC SKIN COLORS AND CAMOUFLAGE, TO DECEIVE THEIR VICTIMS.

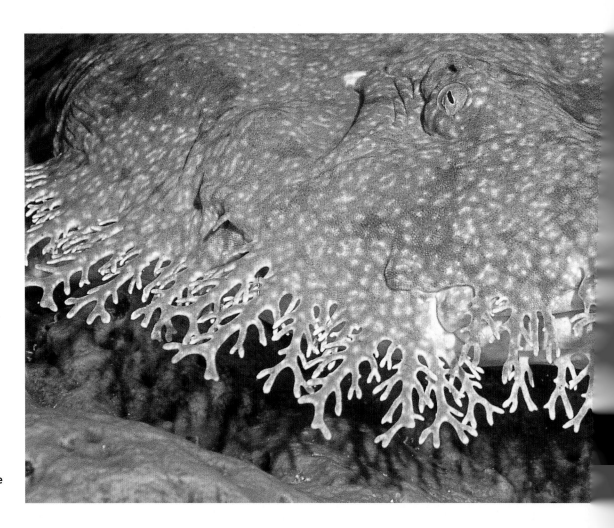

left: "Seaweeds" fringe this rounded sea-bed "boulder"— which is really a frilled wobbegong waiting to open its huge mouth and lunge upwards at its prey.

Shark camouflage involves flaps, frills, and fronds of skin, and even alluring lights in the dark water.

Carpet sharks, the group that includes the wobbegongs, have an excellent skin disguise, with patterns of colorful splotches and spots. These blend in perfectly with the sand, pebbles, and seaweeds on the sea floor. But these sharks also disguise their body outline and sharklike shape. They have frills and fringes of skin around the head and mouth. So they resemble seaweeds and corals not only in color, but also in shape— and even in movement, as the frondlike skin flaps waft in the current, like real seaweed.

The wobbegong lies perfectly still, the only sign of life being its spiracle holes as they open and close for breathing. The shark may even ripple its fronds gently, to catch the attention of a curious crab or fish. As a potential meal approaches to investigate, the "wobby" opens its huge mouth. The influx of water sucks in the hapless victim. As the shark's jaws close, it is trapped within a cage of long, fanglike teeth.

There are several species of wobbegong, living mainly in the seas around Australia and Japan. They include the descriptively named ornate wobbegong, spotted wobbegong, and tasseled wobbegong.

light meals

Deep-sea fish live in a vast and sparsely popu-lated world, where encounters with other creatures are rare and brief. Searching for a meal could take weeks. So many deep-sea species, including some sharks, use glowing lures of light to tempt prey out of the gloom. (Sea anglers at night use bright lamps for the same reason.)

The ability of living things to emit light is called bioluminescence. The glow is produced by special cup-shaped glands, photophores, in the skin. The cells in the gland contain an enzyme (biological catalyst or transforming substance) known as luciferase. This alters a body protein, luciferin, by adding oxygen to it. During the reaction, chemical energy is changed into light energy. A very similar biochemical system has evolved in other creatures, such as glow-worms on land.

The photophore gland is surrounded by transparent microscopic cells that together form a glassy lens, to focus the rays. The "brightest" shark is the cookie-cutter, *Isistius brasiliensis*. It lives in mid-ocean and grows to 20 inches long. In the dark, its lower surfaces glow with an eerie green sheen.

above: **The frilled shark hunts among rocks in deep dark water. Its disguise is mainly dull-colored skin on its back and sides, and a paler underside.**

Another glowing shark is the green dogfish, *Etmopterus virens*. The tiny lantern sharks also have luminous organs scattered over the skin and around the inside of the mouth, to tempt small creatures right inside. The huge megamouth may have a glowing big mouth, or the effect may be due to silvery reflective tissues of mouth lining.

DESIGN FOR LIVING

129

Spines and Spikes

LARGER SHARKS HAVE FEW ENEMIES, AND NEED LITTLE IN THE WAY OF SPECIALIZED DEFENSE.

THEIR FORMIDABLE TEETH ARE MORE THAN ADEQUATE.

But many smaller sharks need strategies to deter attacks from predators—especially bigger sharks.

Most prehistoric sharks had a tall spine or blade standing in front of each of the two dorsal fins. These may have evolved originally to support the fins, in the way that a sailing ship's masts support its sails. The tough, smooth spines were often flattened from side to side, as in *Cladoselache*, or elaborately ridged and lumped. Gradually, internal supports took over, as cartilage rods and dermal rays within the fin developed sufficiently. The spines disappeared. But in some sharks, the spines stayed, and assumed a new role—defense.

Most of the living sharks that possess spines are small bottom-dwellers who use them as protection against attack from above. The majority of species are in the dogfish family, Squalidae. The spiny dogfish or spurdog, *Squalus acanthias*, is caught commercially. Its spines do not protect it from fishing nets, but they can inflict painful wounds on fish-handlers. Each spine bears a groove containing a mild poison. The shark can inject this poison by flicking its body into a curve around the assailant.

The humantin shark, *Oxynotus*, is sometimes called the prickly dogfish. It has not only large spines on its back, but also skin like barbed wire. Horn sharks of the family Heterodontidae, such as the Port Jackson or bullhead shark, also have a stout spine in front of each dorsal fin, which is mildly venomous.

surprise defense

The swellshark is well named from its surprising method of self-defense. If threatened, it suddenly inflates its body to twice the normal size by swallowing air or water. This shark normally

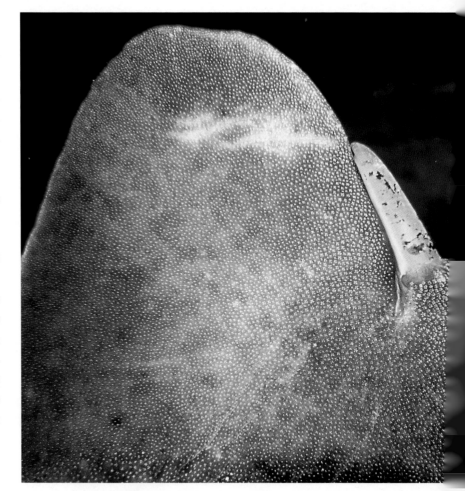

top: **A close-up of a Port Jackson shark's main dorsal fin, showing the defensive spine that can jab a mild toxin into a molester.**

above: **The prehistoric shark, *Tristychius* had a blade standing in front of each dorsal fin.**

DESIGN FOR LIVING

hides by day in a crevice, and if it performs its trick here, it wedges itself in. Held even tighter by its rough skin, it is almost impossible to dislodge. Away from its shelter, the swellshark must rely on startling its attacker by its sudden increase in size, and buying enough time to swim away. However, some swellsharks have been seen floating at the surface for several days, so once the air is swallowed, it may be difficult to expel.

above: **A swellshark eyes the camera and considers whether to bring its defense ploy into full play—suddenly inflating to twice normal size.**

THE GOBLIN SHARK

The grotesque-looking goblin or elfin shark, *Scapanorhynchus*, has a sharp extension like the peak of a cap, protruding from its forehead. This looks like a menacing weapon, but it may simply be a supporting "beam" for extra sensory organs in the skin, to detect prey. The goblin shark was first caught and described for science in the 1880s. Eventually it was recognized as a "living fossil," belonging to a group of sharks that were thought to have died out 100 million years ago.

Skin and Scales

SHARK SKIN HAS BEEN USED FOR CENTURIES, AS A DURABLE, LEATHERY MATERIAL AND AS A SANDPAPER-LIKE ABRASIVE, PROOF OF ITS TOUGHNESS AND STRENGTH.

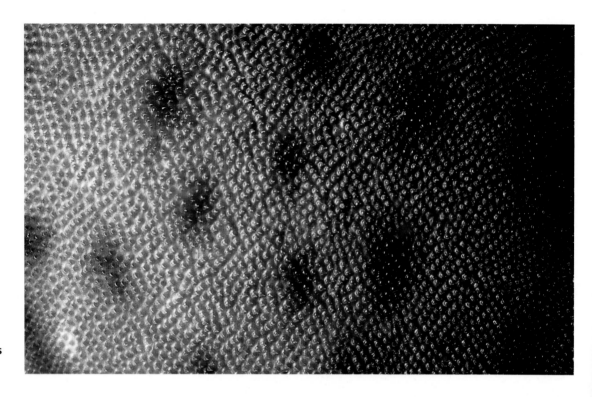

right: **Shark skin scales, or denticles, show up as tiny, tall, narrow-sided pyramids with bent-over points.**

To the shark it's skin is much more than just an ornamental cover. The skin of all vertebrates, from sharks to ourselves, is made up of two layers, the outer epidermis and the inner dermis. The dermis is composed of connective tissue, muscle fibers, sensory nerve cells, and blood capillaries. The epidermis above it consists of dead cells that are produced constantly by the dermis, and which continuously wear away on the outside. It has been discovered that in many species of large shark, the skin is thicker than a human finger. The whale shark's skin is six inches deep, and can reputedly withstand penetration by a harpoon.

skin scales— dermal denticles

The ancestors of the shark were protected by large shieldlike plates embedded in the skin.

Modern sharks no longer have these large plates. But their remnants form dermal denticles—tiny toothlike scales which cover the skin and are unique to sharks. Also called placoid scales, these denticles are very different from the scales of bony fish, and very similar in structure to the shark's actual teeth—indeed, to the teeth of all vertebrates.

A dermal denticle arises in the dermis, anchored by a basal plate. Its point pushes up through the epidermis. A nerve and blood vessel grows through the plate into the soft tissue within the denticle, called the pulp cavity. Around this is a layer of one of nature's hardest substances, dentine. And this is covered by an even harder material, enamel. Once a denticle reaches its full size, it stops growing, eventually falls out, and is replaced by another one. (Just like the shark's teeth—see page 150).

Dermal denticles vary widely in shape and size between shark species. The bramble or briar shark, *Echinorhinus*, has knobbly denticles the size of shirt buttons, each with a tuft of sharp curved thorns in the center. The goblin shark has long thorny denticles, almost the size of the spikes on barbed wire. On other sharks, the denticles are tiny, fractions of an inch long.

On an individual shark, the denticles may vary over the body. Those on the snout are rounded, with nerve connections that assist the sense of touch. Those along the front edges of the fins are diamond-shaped, forming a knife edge to cut through the water. Those on the belly are flatter and shield-shaped, forming a chain-mail suit of armor to protect the skin while the shark is resting on the bottom or feeding.

GOING WITH THE FLOW

Perhaps the most beautifully designed denticles are those along the shark's flanks. Under the microscope, they look like tiny keeled hydrofoils or spoilers, as used on fast boats and cars. This shape probably has more to do with speed than protection. As an object moves through a fluid, it creates eddies, whirls, vortices, and general turbulence. This slows the object's speed and makes movement less energy-efficient.

The shark's denticle design minimizes this problem by directing the water's flow and allowing it to slip by more smoothly, instead of creating turbulence and drag. Possibly the shark can twist and turn the tiny denticles, to cope with individual micro-eddies that its skin sensors detect. Racers of ocean yachts and powerboats can only dream of such an "intelligent hull".

BRAMBLE
SHARK

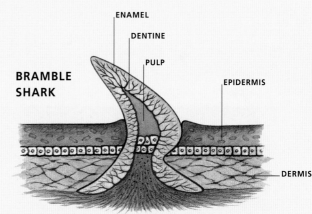

ENAMEL

DENTINE

PULP

BRAMBLE
SHARK

EPIDERMIS

DERMIS

right: **Shark skin scales, or denticles, have the same composition as teeth. The scales serve different functions in various species. Those of the bramble shark (left) are knobbly and prickly and may be for protection and defense. The overlapping keeled scales of the whale shark (middle right) and the ridged scales of gray sharks reduce water resistance.**

GRAY SHARK
(FROM THE REAR)

GRAY SHARK
(FROM ABOVE)

WHALE SHARK
(FROM ABOVE)

Internal Support

THE SHARK SKELETON DOES NOT HAVE TO GIVE THE SAME AMOUNT OF SUPPORT AND

RESISTANCE AGAINST GRAVITY, COMPARED WITH A LAND ANIMAL.

But it has to provide a flexible framework, for the muscles to pull and move. This internal skeleton is made of cartilage, a lightweight, gristly, pearly-translucent, slightly elastic, and pliable substance. It forms the skeletal components, which in engineering terms are levers, beams, rods, and plates, linked by joints to allow the appropriate amounts of movement.

Cartilage is similar to bone. It is not unique to sharks. Skates, rays and rabbitfish have skeletons made of it. Most other vertebrates have skeletons partly made from it, plus some bone. We have it in our own bodies, as flexible supports for the nose and ears, and as a smooth lining over the bones, inside joints. It is composed of fibers of proteins such as collagen and elastin, embedded in a matrix or ground substance of various salts and minerals. It is strong and slightly pliable, yet light—not unlike tough yet "bendy" plastic.

cartilage and bone

The chief difference between cartilage and bone is that bone is cartilage that has been hardened by a process called mineral calcification. This involves crystals of calcium, carbonate, phosphate, and other salts and minerals, which gives extra stiffness, strength, hardness, and brittleness.

Calcification is not absent from a shark's body. It occurs in the vertebrae of the spinal column and in other areas, including the jaws, teeth, fin rods, and dermal denticles or skin scales. It was once believed that sharks lacked bone because they had already evolved along their own course, before true bone appeared in other animals. Now it seems that sharks may have once had more bony skeletons, but they have lost the calcification as a secondary modification.

below: **Viewed from below, this skate (a cartilaginous fish, like sharks) reveals its complex, gristly inner skeleton.**

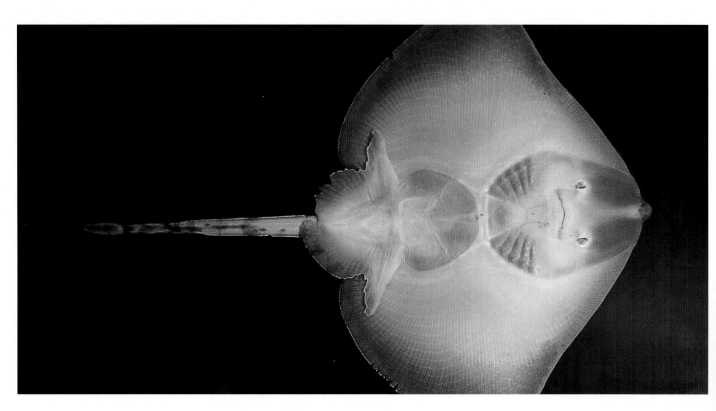

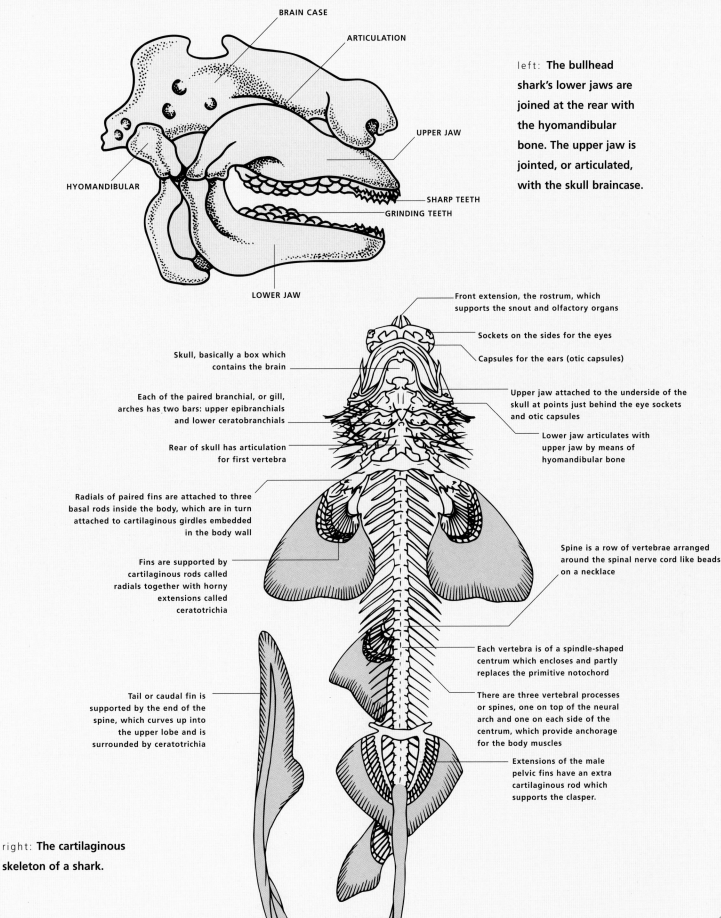

BRAIN CASE

ARTICULATION

UPPER JAW

HYOMANDIBULAR

SHARP TEETH

GRINDING TEETH

LOWER JAW

left: **The bullhead shark's lower jaws are joined at the rear with the hyomandibular bone. The upper jaw is jointed, or articulated, with the skull braincase.**

Skull, basically a box which contains the brain

Each of the paired branchial, or gill, arches has two bars: upper epibranchials and lower ceratobranchials

Rear of skull has articulation for first vertebra

Radials of paired fins are attached to three basal rods inside the body, which are in turn attached to cartilaginous girdles embedded in the body wall

Fins are supported by cartilaginous rods called radials together with horny extensions called ceratotrichia

Tail or caudal fin is supported by the end of the spine, which curves up into the upper lobe and is surrounded by ceratotrichia

Front extension, the rostrum, which supports the snout and olfactory organs

Sockets on the sides for the eyes

Capsules for the ears (otic capsules)

Upper jaw attached to the underside of the skull at points just behind the eye sockets and otic capsules

Lower jaw articulates with upper jaw by means of hyomandibular bone

Spine is a row of vertebrae arranged around the spinal nerve cord like beads on a necklace

Each vertebra is of a spindle-shaped centrum which encloses and partly replaces the primitive notochord

There are three vertebral processes or spines, one on top of the neural arch and one on each side of the centrum, which provide anchorage for the body muscles

Extensions of the male pelvic fins have an extra cartilaginous rod which supports the clasper.

right: **The cartilaginous skeleton of a shark.**

Bending and Flexing

SMALL SHARKS, LIKE THE LEOPARD SHARK, ARE VERY FLEXIBLE AND CAN CURL IN TIGHT BENDS AS THEY WRIGGLE AND GRUB FOR PREY ON THE SEA BED.

Larger sharks like the mako hunt by swimming fast, and their bodies are far less flexible than the leopard shark. Both sharks have the same basic design of skeleton. Like the features on the outside, such as fin shapes and skin color, the shapes of the skeletal components on the inside, and the joints that link them, have been altered by evolution to fit different lifestyles.

Sharks swim with their whole bodies, not just their fins. The bendy, elastic, cartilaginous skeleton is perfect for this type of movement. Some of the joints, such as those between the separate plates that make up the skull, need to be very strong. During the shark's development, fingers of cartilage from each adjacent plate grow between each other, and eventually interlock to form a firm, immovable junction, called a suture. In the skull, sutures between the various curved plates form a fairly rigid box which protects the brain inside.

movable joints

The joints between the vertebrae of the spinal column need to allow slight movement, so the spine can flex and undulate for swimming—but not collapse under the pull of the muscles that are anchored to it. Each vertebra has articulating or joint surfaces with the vertebra in front and behind it—around the edges of its main body, or centrum, and at the top of its upper part, the neural arch.

The joints for the jaws and the branchial arches that support the gills are more flexible, so the shark can open its mouth or its gills wide when necessary. These links are designed like hinges, which allow a great range of movement, but only in one plane or dimension— like a human knee joint. Many sharks also protrude their jaws forwards when they bite (see page 152).

Shark fins were originally wide-based skin flaps. Evolution has changed the shape of the shark and has reduced the base of each pectoral and pelvic fin to a narrower stalk, so the fin can be swiveled or rotated to a degree, and even raised, lowered, and moved back and forth. The many small joints between the fin's basal rods of cartilage and the internal girdles of the skeleton allow this complex range of movement.

left: **A leopard shark "worms" its way along the sea floor. It not so much swims, as wriggles, with its very flexible vertebral (spinal) column—not a back-bone, but a back-cartilage.**

SHARK JOINTS

In the shark skeleton, where one component butts up against another, in a joint, the surfaces in contact are made from extra-smooth cartilage. This reduces wear and tear. There is a shock-absorbing bag of fluid, the synovial capsule, between them, for cushioning and to minimize friction. The ends of the skeletal components are held together by strong, elastic, straplike ligaments. These allow them to move to a degree, but restrict their range of movement and stop them coming apart completely. This whole joint structure is very similar to the joints found in other vertebrates, including mammals such as ourselves.

Muscle Power

They have three main types of muscle tissue:

• Cardiac muscle is found only in the heart. It is specialized to work continually and tirelessly.

• Visceral muscle is found in layers in the internal parts, such as the gullet, guts, excretory and reproductive organs, and blood vessels. It pushes contents through these cavities and tubes, and works under the control of the brain, but largely automatically, on "autopilot."

• Skeletal muscle tissue makes up the muscles that move the skeleton. Their ends are attached to the skeleton's cartilage components and, when the muscles contract, they pull and move the skeleton. This type of muscle tissue is voluntary—that is, it works under direct control of the brain's awareness and will. So the shark can move as it wishes.

On the microscopic level, shark muscles are made of hundreds of hair-fine fibers, called myofibers. In turn, these contain millions of bundles of the threadlike proteins called actin and myosin. These slide past each other with a ratchet-like chemical motion, to make the muscle contract.

moving in waves

Muscles can only pull, they cannot push. So they are arranged in opposing or antagonistic pairs. One pulls to move the body in one direction, while the other relaxes and is stretched. Then the roles are reversed to generate movement in the other direction.

The antagonistic pairs of muscles along a shark's body are on either side of the spinal

below: A great white checks out the diver's yellow gloves, worn specially to tickle its quiet curiosity. Its immensely powerful muscles cause barely a ripple under the skin's smoothness.

column. When they shorten on one side, the corresponding muscles on the opposite side relax, and the spinal column flexes.

The muscle fibers are arranged along the flanks in zigzag blocks called myomeres. The ends of the fibers in each myomere are attached to a sheet of connective material, a tendon called a myosepta, which then connects to the cartilage of the skeleton. There are the same number of myomeres as vertebrae. But their zigzag shapes extend their effect over several vertebrae. This arrangement gives more pull for less energy use.

The myomeres are each attached at two points along the spinal column. When they contract, they pull these two points of the column toward each other, bending it into a wave. Along the row of myomeres, each contracts after the one in front of it, and then relaxes as the one behind the contracts. This sequence produces a curve or wave that travels along the shark, from head to tail. And this is how the shark swims!

TWO TYPES OF MUSCLE

Sharks have two types of skeletal muscle:
• One-tenth of the total is red muscle, in narrow strips along the body's sides, just beneath the skin. Its generous blood supply brings plenty of oxygen, energy-rich sugars, and other nutrients so it can work for long periods without tiring. It is used mainly for the small, smooth movements of cruising.
• The other nine-tenths is white muscle. It has a poorer blood supply and is used in short bursts before tiring. This is why a shark on the attack, making a series of sudden and strenuous motions, may suddenly turn and cruise away. It's tired out.

above: **The starry (or stellate) smooth-hound shark lazily wafts its tail from side to side, saving energy and muscular work by resting regularly on the bottom.**

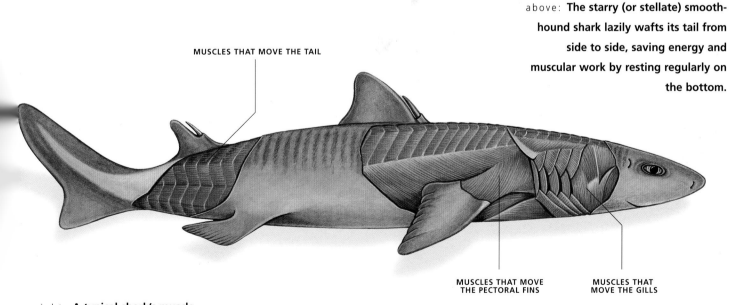

MUSCLES THAT MOVE THE TAIL

MUSCLES THAT MOVE THE PECTORAL FINS

MUSCLES THAT MOVE THE GILLS

right: **A typical shark's muscle system shows the regular zig-zag bands, that contract in waves to flex the body and tail from side to side.**

CHAPTER 6

Design For Killing

Food for Sharks

The oceans provide a wide variety of foods, and sharks have responded by evolving an equally varied set of tastes and food-catching methods.

An ecologist would call a shark a heterotroph. Like nearly all animals, it cannot make its own food, as plants (autotrophs) do. It must feed on food made by other living organisms, at the beginnings of the food chains and webs.

More accurately, sharks are carnivorous heterotrophs. Their food is meat—the flesh of other animals. There are no truly herbivorous or plant-eating sharks. The nearest are the filter-feeders such as the whale, basking, and mega-mouth sharks. They consume the rich "soup" of plankton, which contains a complex mix of tiny floating animals and algae. Virtually all other sharks are hunters—predators who pursue prey.

feed and fast

The carnivore's food of meat usually comes in nutritious packages, which take some time to digest. Carnivores consume food relatively infrequently, compared with many herbivores, who must regularly eat large quantities of nutrient-poor plant food. So after a shark has had a big feed, it fasts while its digestive system breaks down and absorbs the nutrients.

A typical shark takes in, on average, food weighing between 0·5 and 3 percent of its own body weight daily (see page 70). It usually obtains this by feeding on a large meal every two or three days. But it can survive a fast of many weeks, even months, using up the food reserves stored in its relatively huge liver.

Sharks may attack humans, but no shark is designed to specialize in this diet. There were no humans in the sea when shark feeding techniques evolved, millions of years ago. Most shark species are relatively specialized, consuming one main type of food, though some, like the tiger shark, have extremely varied tastes—as shown on the following pages.

previous page: **The great white shark–the ultimate predator.**

left: **Shellfish like the scallop are crunched up by many bottom-dwelling sharks.**

below: **Seabirds like the brown pelican, risk being grabbed from below, pulled under, and swallowed.**

FOOD FOR THOUGHT

- A 10-foot-long captive lemon shark ate an average of 0·5 percent of its total body weight of food every day, but as two or three large meals each week.
- A very large great white shark, weighing a little over a ton, probably consumes about 11 tons of meat in one year. A typical human weighing around 150 pounds consumes about half a ton of food yearly.
- Ten percent of the food that a shark eats goes to make more shark, in the form of growth and maintenance of its own body tissues. The rest of the food is broken down to provide energy for the vital processes of life, including respiration, muscle movement, sending nerve messages, maintaining concentrations of body tissues and fluids, and reproducing.

above left: **Turtles may seem well protected, but a large shark can pierce and crack the strong shell.**

left: **Sea lions make an excellent snack, packed with energy and nutrients, for large predators such as killer whales and big sharks.**

Killer Sharks

MANY LARGE SHARKS ARE PERFECTLY DESIGNED KILLERS. THEIR SUPER-TUNED SENSES HELP THEM TO HOME IN ON FOOD, THEY SWIM POWERFULLY AND SILENTLY TO APPROACH IT, THEIR COLORATION HIDES THEM UNTIL THE LAST SECOND OR TWO, AND THEY ARE EQUIPPED WITH FORMIDABLE TEETH AND JAWS.

Most killer sharks are large because a big body can swim faster than a small one. As most fish in the sea are bony fish, less than 3 feet long, and most killer sharks are a few to several feet long, sharks have the advantage of both size and speed, and surprise.

favored diets

In particular, the mako shark is one of the fastest fish in the ocean. It can reputedly travel at 22–25 miles an hour. It needs to swim at this speed because it feeds on other very swift swimmers, such as tuna, mackerel, and swordfish. The mako's premier technique is to chase and out-swim its prey in a short sprint, bite it hard, and swallow it whole. Failing this, it bites off the victim's tail, and then has a much easier target. One 728-pound mako swallowed a swordfish of 121 pounds—one-sixth of its body weight.

The largest killer shark, the great white, takes the largest prey. It may eat other big fish, such as tuna and other sharks. But it specializes in sea mammals—seals, sea lions, dolphins, and porpoises. Great whites usually bite mouthfuls of flesh from these sizable victims, but they can swallow smaller seals and sea lions, weighing up to 110 pounds and measuring a yard or more long, in one gulp.

Tiger sharks also target large prey such as porpoises, turtles, and other sharks. They are famed for their unfussy tastes and consume crabs, small fish, jellyfish, sea birds and the highly venomous sea-snakes.

Most bottom-dwelling sharks are also killers, although they rely more on stealth than speed to catch their prey.

opposite: **Sharks are naturally curious, nosing and bumping unfamiliar objects to test their edibility.**

above: **A great white seizes the moment— and the meaty bait on a hook and line.**

right: **A tawny shark attacks a sea turtle, biting lumps from the softer, fleshy parts such as tail and limbs.**

When hunting, the shark instinctively assesses the value of a prey item in terms of nourishment, against the energy needed to chase and catch it. This is why most sharks ignore healthy, mature prey animals, which have a good chance of escape. They tend toward easier meat— immature, ill, injured or even dead creatures. In this way, sharks weed out the unfit and poorly adapted from their prey populations, helping to maintain the fitness of ocean communities and drive evolution onward.

A STING-TAILED SNACK

The hammerhead shark specializes on stingrays. It finds them buried in the sand, by sweeping its "metal-detector" hammer-shaped head from side-to-side over the sea bed, to pick up electrical signals, scents, and sounds. When it locates a stingray, it swallows the meal whole, seemingly unbothered by the poisonous spine on the tail. Sometimes the spine sticks permanently in the hammerhead's throat, with apparently no adverse effect.

DESIGN FOR KILLING

Taking Advantage

FEW SHARKS, EVEN THE HIGHLY-TUNED KILLERS, REFUSE A FREE LUNCH. GIVEN THE

OPPORTUNITY, THEY SCAVENGE AND TAKE CARRION.

It is an easy option, being just as nutritious as living prey, but requiring much less energy to catch, and with less risk of fightback and injury.

This tendency to opportunism and scavenging has probably led to the catalog of strange objects found inside shark stomachs, which grows ever longer. The stomachs are usually opened by curious sports anglers, or as part of butchering the shark's carcass for food and materials, or by marine biologists and scientific researchers, or the shark regurgitates its gut contents on being caught, because of stress and as a defense reaction. The list of objects reflects the types of refuse that people throw into the sea, rather than the tastes of sharks.

Perhaps the most notorious underwater scavengers are tiger sharks. Their stomachs have been found to contain:

- A Senegalese native drum
- Lumps of coal
- Cans of paint
- Cigarette packets
- Coats and other items of clothing
- Coils of wire
- Varied pets and livestock, such as dogs, cattle, horses, and chickens
- And of course, parts of human beings …

the murder suspect

In 1935 in Sydney, Australia, a tattooed human arm was regurgitated by a captured tiger shark. Detailed examination showed that the arm had been cut, not by the shark's teeth, but with a blade of some sort—a murder had been committed. A suspect was arrested for killing and dismembering the victim, who was identified from the tattoo, in a case that became known as the "Shark Arm Murder." The tiger shark was acquitted as merely an innocent scavenging accomplice.

Blue sharks, among others, follow ships at sea. Like seagulls that do the same in the air above, the sharks undoubtedly anticipate a free meal, when the ship jettisons its garbage, leftovers, and out-of-condition food supplies. One gray shark, 10 feet long, was found to have eaten eight legs of mutton, half a ham, the back end of a pig, and the front half of a dog, complete with collar and lead. Plus about 300 pounds of horse meat, a barnacle-scraper for the ship's hull, and a piece of sacking.

above: **Gray reef sharks circle a whale carcass, occasionally swimming in to tear off another lump.**

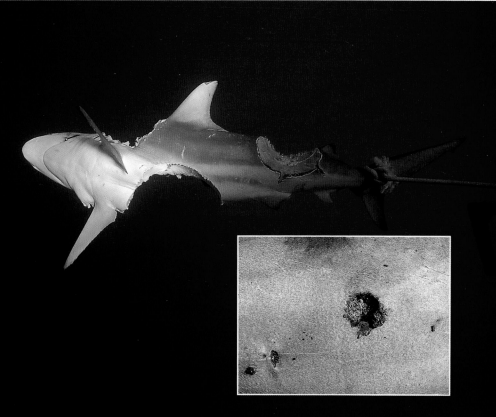

right: **This reef shark is a victim of one of its cousins—a huge bull shark who bit out neat chunks.**

THE PARASITE SHARK

A parasite is a living thing that gains food and/or shelter at the expense of another living thing, the host, causing it harm in the process. The only known parasitic shark is the cookie-cutter. It is only about 19 inches long, but its hosts are much larger animals, including seals, whales, dolphins, and fish. The cookie-cutter swims in the deep sea by day, but comes near the surface at night. It might attract its host with its luminous organs, and when close enough, it opens its mouth wide and sucks itself on to the host's side, though no one knows this for sure. The jaws, edged with large serrated teeth, form a perfect cookie-cutter, as used by cooks in the kitchen. The shark closes its lower jaw, twists its body around, and slices out a half-ball of flesh, like an ice-cream scoop. The host is not killed, but is probably left feeling very sore, and its flesh is open to infection.

left: **The cookie-cutter, relies on stealth as it darts in to nip lumps out of bigger creatures with its "pastry-cutter" jaws.**

inset above: **The wound left by a cookie-cutter shark, after it scooped a mouthful of flesh from this elephant seal.**

Big Sharks, Small Food

EVEN FAIRLY CLEAR SEA WATER CONTAINS SUSPENDED EDIBLE BITS AND PIECES, INCLUDING THE TINY PLANTS AND ANIMALS OF THE PLANKTON, EGGS AND IMMATURE LARVAE OF FISH AND CRABS AND OTHER CREATURES, AND BITS OF FLOATING DEBRIS AND DETRITUS.

This "sea soup" provides food for basking sharks in cold seas, whale sharks in warm seas, and megamouth sharks by night.

Filter-feeding is one of the oldest and most widely used methods of acquiring nourishment in the sea, used by animals as varied as sponges, worms, clams and sea lilies. Far back in evolutionary time, the earliest fish were probably filter-feeders. Today the gills of the whale, basking, and megamouth sharks have returned to their original food-filtering function. They strain the plankton from the water flowing over them, and in the process also catch small fish, shrimps, krill, and other creatures who are consuming the plankton.

The three shark species are ram-type filter-feeders. They swim through their food with their huge mouths open, straining out the particles with the comb-like rakers on their gills. The concentration of plankton in sea water varies enormously, but on average is around one fluid ounce in more than 7,800 gallons. So the filter-feeders must sift huge volumes of water to gather any appreciable weight of food. A basking shark cruising at two knots filters about 528,000 gallons of water, and extracts about 4½ pounds of food from it, each hour.

The basking shark swims slowly through the plankton for a minute or so, then closes its mouth and swallows the food. Whale sharks can augment their diet by actively sucking in schools of small fish, such as anchovies, which are feeding on the plankton.

how the filters work

The filtering apparatus of these sharks occupies a large proportion of the body, with the head being more than one-quarter of the creature's whole length. The gill arches are extended upward and downward to form almost an entire circle around the throat region. Basking shark rakers are close-set rows of bristles about four inches long, between the gill arches. The whale shark's rakers have meshlike spongy tissue. In both species, there are copious amounts of sticky slime or mucus coated on the gills, to aid the filtration process.

The tiny food particles are thought to be trapped in four ways. Some are simply too big to pass through the gaps. Some stick to the mucus. Some are swirled on to the bristles as the stream of water rushes past, a process called interstitial impaction. And some simply sink, owing to gravity, and land on the filters.

below: **Microscopic organisms teem in their billions in the sea, even in seemingly clear water. They are the basis of the food chains which nourish larger animals.**

below: **The gill arches, with their comb-like gill rakers, are visible inside the cavernous mouth of this basking shark.**

right: **Well-preserved megamouth or "big-mouth" sharks, like this specimen in a Los Angeles museum, are exceptionally rare.**

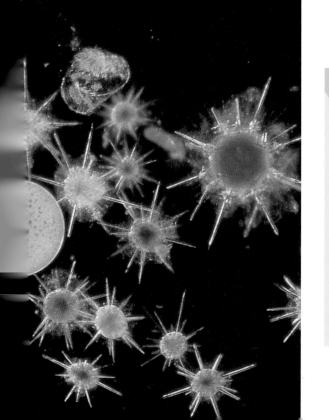

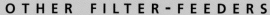

OTHER FILTER-FEEDERS

- There are about 20 species of ocean fish, such as herrings, sardines, anchovies, and mackerel, which have gill-rakers and filter-feed on tiny particles of plankton.
- So do the largest of all rays, the mantas or devilfish.
- The great whales also feed in this way, with their fringed, comb-like plates of baleen (whalebone), designed for bigger items such as finger-sized, shrimp-like krill.
- And in fresh water, so do creatures ranging from frog tadpoles to flamingos and dabbling ducks.

The Teeth of the Shark

THE SHARK'S ULTIMATE LETHAL WEAPONS, FOR ATTACK, FEEDING AND DEFENSE, ARE ITS TEETH. THESE CONSTANTLY GROW AND REPLACE THEMSELVES, SO THEY ARE ALWAYS BRAND-NEW, RAZOR-SHARP, AND READY FOR ACTION.

The typical shark's teeth are enlarged versions of the skin scales or dermal denticles that cover its body (see page 132). Each tooth is made of the hard but slightly pliable, shock-absorbing substance called dentine. This is covered by an outer layer of even harder enamel. In the tooth's center is the pulp chamber or cavity, with blood vessels and nerves. Some sharks have as many as 3,000 teeth, others only a few dozen.

The bases of the teeth, called the roots or feet, are not anchored in the jaw cartilages. They sit in a fibrous mass, the tooth bed, which in turn sits on the jaw cartilage and is held in place by the fleshy gum.

The teeth are arranged in rows, which move slowly forward, like a conveyor-belt system, from the rear inside of the jaw, around to the front outside. Usually only the front one or two rows are functional, in biting. As they wear and fall out or break off, a new row moves from behind, to take their place. This replacement happens about every two weeks, the new teeth lying in wait beneath a skinlike membrane, until they "erupt" and come into use.

The tooth-replacement process starts even as a shark develops in its egg case or mother. And it continues until death. So a shark may get through as many as 20,000 teeth in its lifetime.

variations on the dental theme

The shapes of shark teeth reflect the types of food that each species eats (see panel). They vary from long, thin, pointed awls for catching fast, slippery fish and squid, to serrated or fluted triangular blades for cutting through and sawing off chunks of flesh, to flat millstones for grinding shellfish and crabs out of their shells. In

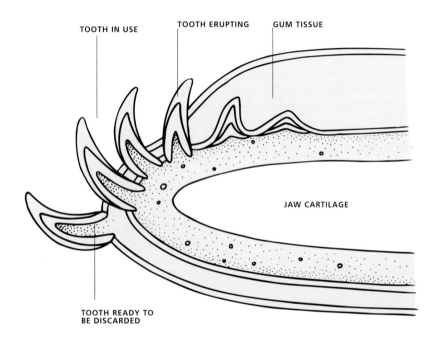

above: **Shark teeth grow on the inner surface of the jaw, beneath the gum tissue. As they move forward, they erupt or appear above the gum, then pass over the jawbone as they are used, and break off.**

TOOTH IN USE   TOOTH ERUPTING   GUM TISSUE

JAW CARTILAGE

TOOTH READY TO BE DISCARDED

addition, some species have different shapes of teeth in different parts of the mouth, to cope with a variety of foods. Also, tooth shape may change through life, as the young shark, which takes smaller, easy-to-catch prey, grows and moves on to larger, more difficult food items. In some species, such as the banded cat shark *Halaelurus*, teeth vary between the sexes. The males use their small front teeth to nibble the females during courtship.

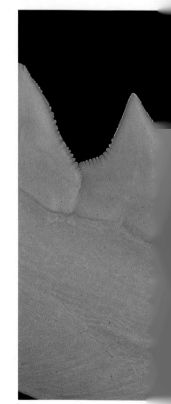

right: **The thin, pointed, blade-like teeth of a bull shark were the natural forerunners of our own purpose-designed sawblades.**

DESIGN FOR KILLING

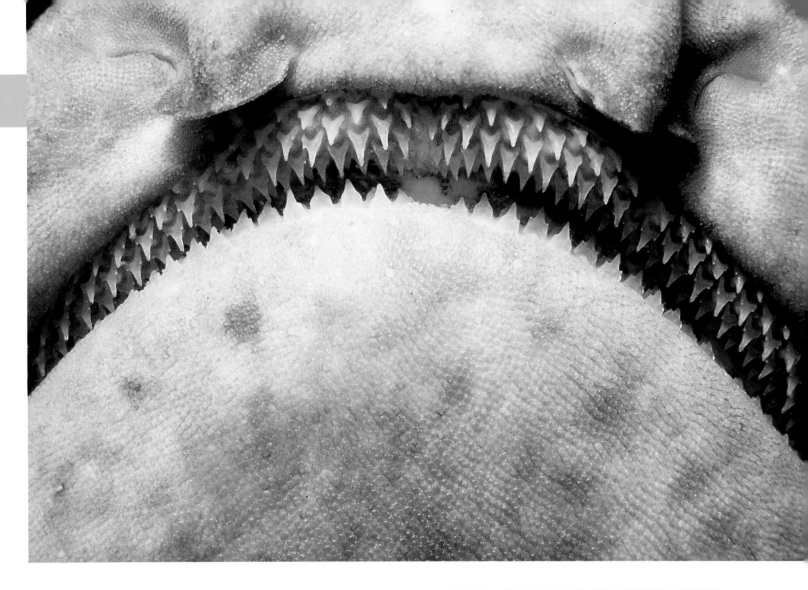

above: **Rows of teeth await their turn, as they march slowly to the edges of the shark's jaws.**

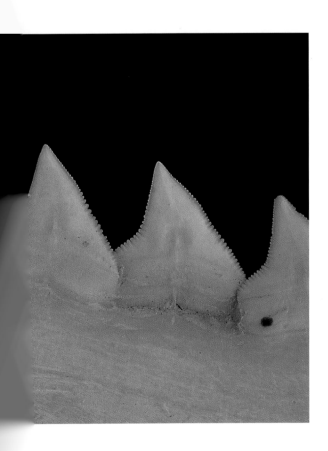

- *Whale shark* Filter-feeds on plankton with gill-rakers, also has hundreds of tiny teeth arranged in 300 rows, with 10 or 15 rows operating at any one time, to form a rasp.
- *Bull shark* Eats almost anything it can catch, using "steak-knife" teeth with serrated edges.
- *Port Jackson shark* Eats shellfish, has rasplike teeth at the front of the jaws and flat, grinding teeth at the back.
- *Porbeagle* Eats fish and shellfish, using three or four rows of slender awl-like teeth with small, sharp cusps at the bases.
- *Great white* Eats tuna and sea mammals, has triangular, serrated-edged teeth just under half an inch long.
- *Smooth-hound, nurse shark* Eat shellfish, have a "pavement" of flat, slablike, crushing teeth.
- *Goblin shark* Eats deep-sea bottom-dwelling creatures, has some long, thornlike teeth and some shorter teeth.
- *Tiger shark* Eats anything, has teeth with narrow, sharp tips and wide, scallop-fluted bases.
- *Swell shark* Eats small fish, has tiny, sharp teeth.
- *Sand tiger* Eats fish and some types of shellfish, using long, narrow, curved teeth.

Jaw Power

"JAWS" IS A VERY APT NAME FOR A SHARK. THE TEETH WOULD BE ALMOST USELESS WITHOUT STRONG JAWS AND POWERFUL JAW MUSCLES, TO GIVE THEM REAL BITE.

above: **The sand tiger shark's teeth are equipped with twin "prongs" or cusps at the base, and a long dagger-like blade.**

right: **The curved jaw of this blue shark shows how its teeth are wide triangles when seen from the side, yet almost razor-thin when seen edge-on.**

Indeed, jaws were the original reason for the evolutionary success of sharks.

At first sight, the jaws of an open-ocean predatory shark, like the mako or great white, do not appear to be ideally positioned for the job of hunting. They are slung awkwardly underneath the protruding snout, rather than being at the front of a more flattened face, as in land predators such as lions and tigers. The ancient Greek naturalist and philosopher Aristotle recognized this difficulty, and assumed that the shark must turn upside down, on its back, in order to attack and feed.

Evolution has overcome this apparent design fault by making both the lower and upper jaws of the shark separate from its skull, attached only by elastic ligaments and stretchy muscles. When it bites, the great white shark tilts its head up and back, and pushes or protrudes both jaws forward, as it opens its mouth. It strikes with the lower jaw first, stabbing the victim with the longer, narrower teeth there. Then the upper jaw bites downward onto the victim, so that its wider, bladelike teeth can shear off a slice of flesh. The rest of the shark's head and body is protected from the power of the impact and bite by an elaborate system of shock-absorbing joints around the skull and spinal column.

the strength of bite

Sharks' bite strengths have been measured scientifically, using a device called a gnatho-dynamometer—*gnatho* relating to jaws. This is basically a plastic or metal ring, whose hardness is accurately known (though there are many more sophisticated designs). It is put inside a piece of fish as bait, the shark bites it, the teeth indent the metal, the indentations are measured, and the strength of the jaws, in terms

of pressure—force per unit area—is calculated. The bite of a big shark has been recorded at three tonnes per square centimetre. This works out to around 132 pounds per tooth.

Sharks like the great white, which sometimes feed on prey that is too big to swallow whole, need to bite off chunks. Their teeth are effective blades, which mesh and lock together almost perfectly when the jaws close, with hardly any gap. But this means the shark cannot shear and slide its jaws from side to side, to complete the cut. So the shark shakes its whole head rapidly from side to side. The teeth work like saw blades, slicing sideways through the flesh, and the meaty lump soon comes away, ready for swallowing.

Some shark species do not need a powerful, cutting bite. They eat crabs, clams, and similar smallish, hard-shelled items, which need grinding up. The upper jaw of the Port Jackson shark is held to the skull by tough ligaments, while the bottom jaw is supported by a separate structure, the hyomandibular cartilage. This arrangement allows the top and bottom jaws to move against each other, forward and backward and sideways. So the flat teeth inside form a powerful grinding mill.

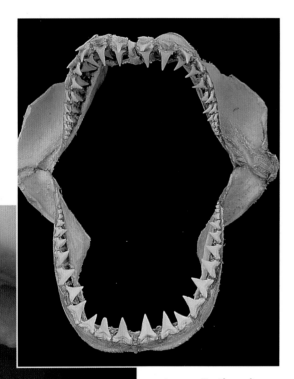

above: **Teeth and jaws of the biggest predatory shark, the great white. The wide jaw flanges anchor the powerful biting muscles.**

top right: **Teeth of another big meat-eater, and one of the largest predators ever to walk on earth—the dinosaur** *Tyrannosaurus.*

BITE STRENGTHS COMPARED

Using various semiscientific and occasionally devious means, biologists have been able to measure the bite pressures of different animals. This includes even the long-gone dinosaur *Tyrannosaurus rex*, working from the fossilized bite indentations on the bones of one of its favorite prey, the three-horned dinosaur *Triceratops horridus*.

ANIMAL	RELATIVE BITE STRENGTH
Tyrannosaurus	13,400
Alligator	13,000
Great white shark	9,000
Lion	4,100
Orangutan	1,700
Dusky shark	1,600
Wolf	1,500
Human	600
Labrador dog	500

Food Breakdown

MOST SHARKS CANNOT CHEW IN ORDER TO SOFTEN THEIR FOOD AND BEGIN ITS PHYSICAL BREAKDOWN OR DIGESTION.

They swallow smaller victims whole, or bite off and swallow smaller pieces of larger victims. So the shark needs a strong, effective digestive system, to break down these lumps of food both physically and chemically, into molecule-sized pieces that can be absorbed from the guts, into the shark's body, for its own life processes.

The digestive tract is basically a long tube, from mouth to cloaca. Some parts, like the stomach, are wider than others. Physical digestion starts in the mouth. The jaws and teeth seize the food, gill rakers lining the insides of the gill arches prevent a struggling prey from escaping, and the mouth lining produces a slimy mucus to ease the passage of the food into the throat.

The jaws and the muscles of the throat push the food back farther, where it is swallowed by waves of contractions passing along the short, narrow, muscular gullet, or esophagus. This leads into a U-shaped storage bag for the meal—the stomach. The first arm of the U is called the cardiac limb (since it is near the heart). The second arm is the pyloric limb, leading onward to the intestine.

shark stomach

The typical shark stomach is loose-walled and very stretchy. This allows for massive expansion, so the creature can take advantage of a plentiful meal. Microscopic glands in the stomach lining produce powerful gastric juices, which contain strong hydrochloric acid and also an enzyme or chemical convertor, pepsin. This begins the chemical breakdown of body proteins in the meaty prey. Gastric juices are produced under the control of nerve signals from the brain and hormones circulating in body fluids, in response to the sight, sound, or smell of food. So when the shark swallows, its stomach is ready and waiting to digest.

As explained on page 146, many sharks are opportunistic scavengers. They swallow all kinds of objects that happen to come their way. But the shark's stomach has a trick to get rid of unsuitable, indigestible or unwanted bits and pieces that it has consumed. It can evert, or push itself almost inside out, back up the gullet and into the throat. In this way, troublesome stomach contents can be forcibly regurgitated and ejected through the mouth. We have a similar mechanism in our bodies—vomiting.

Sharks regurgitate not only unsuitable objects, but also as a means of self-defense. The cloud of fragments emerging from the mouth distracts or repels any creature harassing or threatening the shark. For some predators, it offers an alternative meal, second-best to the shark itself.

below: **Sharks take just seconds to feed, but days to digest.**

bottom: **A well-fed shark stores digested food mainly in its liver.**

BREAK DOWN, BUILD UP

As food passes along the digestive tract, it is attacked by strong digestive juices, acids, and enzymes. These break down large, complex molecules in the food into their smaller, simpler component units. For example, proteins are chopped into amino acids, starches, or carbohydrates into sugars, and fats or lipids into fatty acids and glycerol. This breaking down of food is called chemical digestion. The simple component molecules are small enough to pass through the tract lining, into the shark's blood and body tissues. They are used as building blocks for growth and repair, and as energy sources for running body systems and movement. These myriad chemical reactions within the tissues are called metabolism.

Shark Guts

AFTER A SHARK SWALLOWS ITS MEAL, THE FOOD STAYS IN THE STOMACH FOR MANY HOURS, EVEN DAYS, AS IT IS DIGESTED CHEMICALLY BY ACIDS, ENZYMES, AND OTHER POWERFUL JUICES.

below: The digestive system of a shark is relatively short, compared to other vertebrates, but the stomach is hugely expandable. The spiral valve in the intestine provides an enormous surface area for digestion.

CARDIAC LIMB

PYLORIC LIMB

PHARYNX

ANUS/CLOACA

RECTUM

SPIRAL VALVE

INTESTINE

STOMACH

OESOPHAGUS

MOUTH

below: A bronze whaler could cruise for weeks after one big meal.

A shark's swallowed food is prevented from moving onward from the stomach into the next region of the digestive tract—the intestines —by a ring of muscle, the pyloric sphincter. Gradually, as digestion continues, this ring relaxes at intervals, and allows the semidigested food to dribble into the intestines. The food is propelled by waves of muscular contractions, called peristalsis, along the walls of the tract.

Two multipurpose glands manufacture yet more digestive juices, and empty them along tubes into the intestine. One is the liver, which makes bile fluids to break down and digest all kinds of components and nutrients in the food, especially fats and oils. The liver has many other vital roles in digestion and body chemistry, including storage of the results of digestion, such as sugars, starches, and fats, and breaking down old, worn-out cells in the blood. This organ, lying below the stomach and in front of the heart, almost between the pectoral fins, is especially large in sharks.

The second organ, just behind the liver, is the pancreas. It is both an endocrine gland, produc-ing the chemical messengers called hormones for coordination of body processes, and an exocrine gland, producing many powerful digestive enzymes that break down proteins, fats, and starches in the food.

unique to sharks

The shark's intestine not only continues the digestive or breakdown process, but also begins to absorb the products. The best design to do this has a very large internal surface area, for maximum absorption. Many animals, including ourselves, have solved this problem by having a very long intestine, looped and coiled within the body. But sharks have a very short, wide intestine, containing a structure unique to their group—the spiral valve.

The spiral valve is actually a helix shape, more like a screw. It is composed of a shelflike outfold of the intestinal wall, which is twisted round and round, as many as 40 times. This increases the surface area of the lining within the intestine for better absorption of digested nutrients.

The spiral valve design varies in different types of shark. In the hammerhead, it looks more like a scroll, or roll of paper. In the dogfish, it resembles a series of stacked cones, piled with the point of one inside the wide base of the next. In the megamouth shark, it looks like a wide "spiral" (helical) staircase.

After the intestine with its spiral valve, the next stage of the digestive tract is the rectum or hind gut. It is short and wide, and has an adjacent gland, the rectal gland, sometimes called the "third kidney." This filters wastes from the blood and empties them into the rectum. The rectum in turn empties all the digestive wastes into the cloaca, where they meet products from the kidneys and reproductive organs. The cloaca opens to the outside via a slit in the shark's rear underside, usually just behind the pelvic fins, called the vent.

above: **A horn shark looks inactive, but inside, its intestines are busy with chemical digestion.**

CORKSCREW FECES

As the remnants of leftovers and undigested food pass through the spiral valve, forming into semisolid digestive wastes or feces, they take on the valve's shape. So the "design" of shark feces is characteristic of the species of shark. Feces that have fossilized and turned to stone, called coprolites, are likewise shaped. They give clues to the guts and internal structure of long-extinct prehistoric sharks.

Do Sharks Hunt in Packs?

They hunt in packs or teams, cooperating with each other to maximize the chances of catching prey, so that they each obtain more food than they could if hunting alone. Recent observations of shark behavior are revealing more and more evidence that sharks can also organize themselves and cooperate as group predators.

Some sharks congregate to feed, merely because food is there; there is little interaction. Each feeds in its own way, oblivious of its fellows, apart from minor squabbles when two sharks try to eat the same food item. This seems to explain why whale sharks and basking sharks gather in groups of 20 or more, to take advantage of a rich area of plankton.

Spiny dogfish, or spurdogs, sometimes gather in huge shoals and sweep along the sea bed, driving all living things before them, like the shark version of army ants. Any animal that cannot escape is consumed. Each of the sharks is constantly watching its fellows, as well as looking out for its own food. When one finds something edible, others notice its behavior and rapidly congregate at the site, to see if there is more. Many types of birds feed in this way, as flocks hopping across a field, all searching for a meal but also watching each other. Gathering at a feeding site, in response to the behavior of others of the same species, is perhaps the first step toward cooperative hunting.

hunting packs

It is very difficult to observe and understand the behavior of sharks in groups, but a few species of sharks may, at times, hunt cooperatively, in packs. Indeed, sharks such as smooth-hounds and dogfish are so named because they are usually found prowling in large packs, like wild dogs. This has the advantage of enabling smaller sharks to catch and feed on larger prey, with less expenditure of effort. The end result may seem similar to the group hunting of dogs or lions, but in these sharks, the behavior is based more on sets of instinctive or inborn responses, rather than on intelligent planning, decision-making and learned experience.

However, a few sharks show behavior that is hard to explain as merely instinctive. Sand sharks or great whites may spread out around their intended prey, such as a shoal of fish. The sharks then swim inward together, from several

below: **Dozens of hammerhead sharks gather in a school circling an underwater hilltop near the Cocos Islands, in the Pacific.**

different directions, herding the fish into a tight knot. Thresher sharks do this by working in pairs, thrashing the fish together with their long tails.

As the fish shoal is kept together in a dense mass by the circling pack, one shark at a time comes in for a mouthful. This behavior can continue for several minutes, until the shoal of fish becomes too small and is no longer worth the effort. Some observers say that two or three great white sharks may even form "friendships." Not only do they hunt cooperatively when the opportunity arises, but they also take turns and share the proceeds equally.

LITTLE SHARKS, BIG PREY

Green dogfish prowl in large shoals, in deep water. These little sharks, only 10 inches long, are numerous enough to tackle large octopus and squid. No one has filmed their kill, but presumably the only way they could overcome such large prey is by swarming around it en masse, biting out chunks with their savage teeth, in the manner of piranhas in fresh water. During the attack, intelligent communication between the sharks is unlikely, but they remain in instinctive contact, using their luminescent organs.

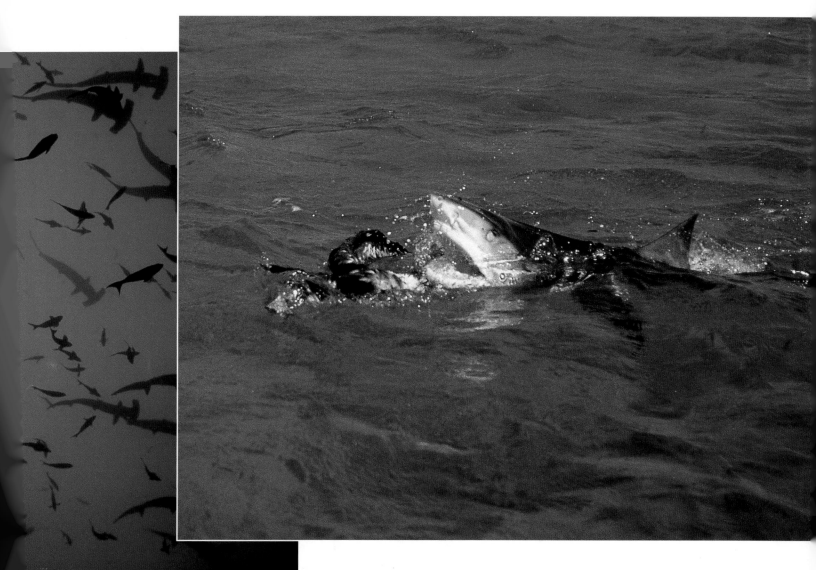

above: **As young seabirds such as this albatross leave the nest, sharks gather to feast.**

The Feeding Frenzy

SOME SHARKS SEEM TO GO COMPLETELY OUT OF CONTROL AT FEEDING TIME. THE PRESENCE OF FOOD DRIVES THEM INTO A FRENZY OF WHIRLING, THRASHING BODIES, AND THE SHARKS SEEM AS LIKELY TO TAKE CHUNKS OUT OF EACH OTHER AS OUT OF THE PREY.

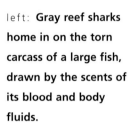

left: **Gray reef sharks home in on the torn carcass of a large fish, drawn by the scents of its blood and body fluids.**

below: **Bronze whalers feed in a frenzy of thrashing tails and fins—their own and their victims'.**

Sharks do not seem to feed in response to pangs of hunger, as we try to do, when there is no food in the stomach. There are many examples of some sharks eagerly swallowing bait when their digestive systems are already stuffed full of food, and other sharks in aquaria whose digestive systems must be almost empty, yet they remain uninterested in a suitable meal for days, possibly even weeks. It appears, instead, that sharks have a continuous low-level drive or motivation to feed.

If a shark is in a generally unaroused state, cruising gently on "autopilot," it may make a half-hearted effort to grab a passing injured fish, or to investigate a possible meal by nudging it with its snout.

However, when a shark detects food, by sound or scent or other sense, or it detects other sharks feeding, then this casual, low-level behavior changes into a heightened state of arousal. The shark swims more actively and is now likely to bite earnestly at anything around. Perhaps it knows instinctively that any moments lost in exploratory nudges or lethargic test bites could now mean that another shark might steal the food.

escalating excitement

As more sharks are attracted to the scene, tension mounts and excitement levels escalate. Each shark becomes so aroused that it begins to slash at the others, possibly in attempts to drive away any competition for the meal. As injuries occur and blood begins to flow, the frenzy builds further. The original food source may now be long gone, yet the sharks continue, and begin to take chunks out of each other. Such a seething *mêlée* can strip flesh from skeletons in seconds. Furthermore, the sharks cannot be put off—even explosions of TNT have failed to interrupt such an orgy of consumption.

Are these feeding frenzies a natural phenomenon? They generally occur near fishing boats, when the catch is hauled in. Such a dense concentration of injured and struggling fish, trapped in a net, is hardly natural. And the results are devastating for the fishing crew. Even more horrendous are reports of shark feeding frenzies at shipwrecks, where people are consumed. Again, a group of humans in mid-ocean is hardly a natural occurrence. Perhaps the sharks are responding to what biologists call a "supernormal stimulus"—a situation that they have not encountered in their millions of years of evolution, but that triggers off normal inborn sets of instincts and motivations, to a highly abnormal level. Put simply, without realizing, they overreact.

Some observers contend that a certain level of feeding frenzy is a natural phenomenon. It sometimes occurs in shallow waters, where large numbers of young sea birds, seals, or sea lions are entering the water and learning to swim for the first time. Many sharks gather, thrash about and eat until almost bursting.

CHAPTER 7

More Sharks— or Fewer?

Strategies and Threats

SHARKS HAVE A REPUTATION AS "PRIMITIVE" ANIMALS, THE CREATURES THAT TIME FORGOT,

LEFT OVER FROM THE MISTS OF PREHISTORY.

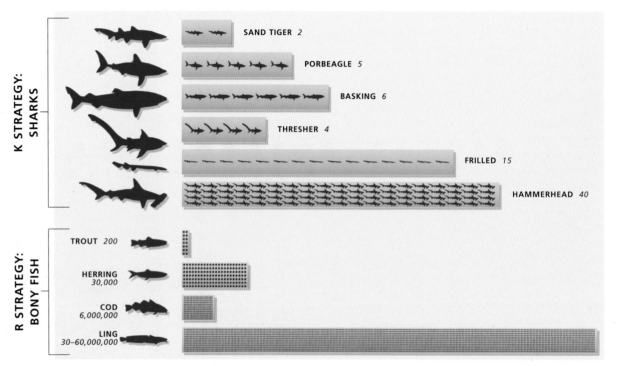

K STRATEGY: SHARKS

SAND TIGER 2
PORBEAGLE 5
BASKING 6
THRESHER 4
FRILLED 15
HAMMERHEAD 40

R STRATEGY: BONY FISH

TROUT 200
HERRING 30,000
COD 6,000,000
LING 30–60,000,000

left: **Many sharks use the "K strategy" of reproduction, with few but well-provisioned offspring, compared to the "R strategy" of bony fish. The chart shows the typical number of young certain types of shark bear in one season compared with bony fish, using the "R strategy".**

The very fact of the shark's continuing survival means that evolution has made them as modern and up to date as any other living thing, in all respects—their shape, cartilage skeleton, teeth and jaws, their behavior, and, of course, their reproduction.

The way that sharks breed is far from simple or primitive. It shows features that are far more advanced, in evolutionary terms, than the reproductive methods of bony fish. In some cases, shark reproduction is almost as sophisticated as the mammalian system, where babies develop inside the mother and are born fully formed.

Biologists recognize two basic strategies for reproduction. One is the animal that puts all its energies and resources into producing huge numbers of eggs. There are so many eggs produced that any form of parental care is impossible, so the eggs are simply left alone to hatch, and the young develop at the mercy of the environment.

The chances of any single youngster surviving are very poor, but by the law of averages, hopefully one or two make it to maturity and breed. This is called the R strategy and is followed by many bony fish. A female cod, for example, produces some 3 million eggs, while a female ling may release 20 million. The male partners simply cast their sperm into the sea near the eggs, leaving fertilization to chance.

few young, but a good start

The second option is the K strategy. The animal puts its reproductive energies and resources into producing relatively few young, but giving these a very high chance of survival, with a good start in life. Most mammals have this strategy, with few young developing in the female's uterus (womb). Monkeys, apes, elephants, whales, and dolphins take it even further, with extended periods of parental care after birth.

opposite above: **On average, the sand tiger shark has only two young per season.**

previous page: **The egg case of a dogfish, the embryo is attached to the yolk store.**

MORE SHARKS—OR FEWER?

The R and K strategies are not widely separate, but two ends of a range or spectrum. Many creatures are somewhere in the middle. Humans are one of the most extreme K types. Sharks, too, tend very much toward the K end. Rather than casting eggs and sperm into the sea, they have mating and internal fertilization, where sperm fertilize the eggs inside the female's body. The few eggs have thick, protective cases and large reserves of yolk, so the young can develop to an advanced stage. In some sharks, the eggs are laid carefully in specially selected nursery areas. In other species, they are retained inside the mother's body and hatch there, so the young sharks are born fully formed, well equipped for an independent existence.

COPING WITH CHANGE

The K-type reproductive strategy ensures success while conditions and the environment are unvarying and stable. But it is a slow method of breeding, which makes it less able to cope with dramatic change. Sharks reach maturity only after several years of growth. They may breed only every two or more years, with a few young each time. When conditions alter rapidly—disease changes in the environment, increased persecution from humans—the population tends to fall quickly. The slow reproductive rate means that numbers recover slowly, too—or even not at all.

The Males of the Species

THE ESSENTIAL ROLE OF THE MALE SHARK IS TO INSEMINATE THE FEMALE, PASSING HIS SPERM INTO HER BODY, TO FERTILIZE HER EGGS.

above: **This is a male great white, as evidenced by his two finger-shaped claspers on the rear underside.**

During the breeding season, males take a break from the routine activities of feeding, and set off in search of mates.

Inside the male shark's body are two long reproductive glands, the testes. In most species they are in the upper middle body, just below and in front of the main dorsal fin. Besides making the microscopic, tadpole-shaped male sex cells, or sperm, the testes are also part of the hormonal system. They secrete hormones which control the development of male bodily features and characteristics, such as the growth of the claspers. Hormones also control the shark's

yearly breeding cycle, and initiate the urge to mate or copulate.

The male shark produces sperm cells from the testes, which pass along a tube toward the common opening for digestive, excretory, and reproductive materials—the cloaca. The first part of the tube is called the vas efferentia, and the second part is the vas deferens. Glands in its lining make a sticky mucus-like substance that binds millions of the tiny sperm into bundles or packets, known as spermatophores. These then pass into a storage bag, the seminal vesicle, until the shark mates.

claspers that do not clasp

The main external difference between a male and female shark, apart from the female's greater body size, is that the male has claspers. These appendages are formed from the inner sides of the pelvic fins, which are rolled around in a scroll-like fashion. They were named by the ancient Greek "father of natural history," Aristotle, who assumed that the male shark used them to grasp and hold the female in a mating embrace during copulation. But Aristotle was mistaken. Like a male mammal's penis, they are really sperm channels for placing the sperm into the female's body.

Known scientifically as myxopterygia, the claspers are stiffened by cartilaginous rods. They contain erectile tissue, which enlarges and stiffens when engorged with blood, for mating. Each clasper has a mechanism for pumping the sperm, in their spermatophore packages, through the channel at the center of the scroll. There is also a hole in each clasper near the cloaca, called the apopyle (see page 172), and two siphon sacs lying under the skin nearby, in the anal region. These sacs are believed to secrete lubricating fluid into the apopyle and over the claspers, to reduce friction during copulation. The sacs also contain sea water, which is used to help wash the sperm into the female's body.

the variety of claspers

Just like their owners, the claspers of male sharks have a range of sizes and shapes. They may be flat, round, smooth, or covered with hook- or spurlike denticles. They are small in juveniles, reaching their full size only at maturity. However, from this stage, they do not get any bigger through life—though the rest of the shark does. So old, large males have proportionally smaller claspers.

above: **A closer view of the male claspers, on a juvenile yago shark from the Red Sea.**

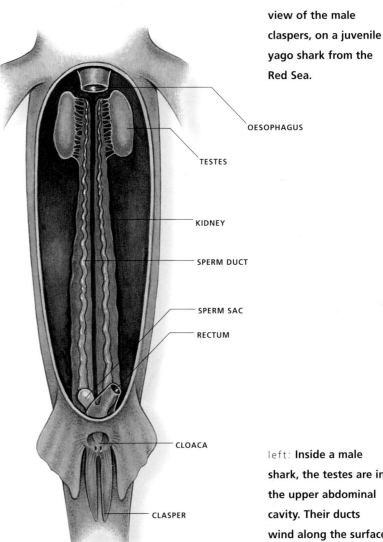

OESOPHAGUS

TESTES

KIDNEY

SPERM DUCT

SPERM SAC

RECTUM

CLOACA

CLASPER

left: **Inside a male shark, the testes are in the upper abdominal cavity. Their ducts wind along the surface of the kidneys, carrying sperm to the sperm sacs.**

The Females of the Species

THE FEMALE SHARK'S MAIN REPRODUCTIVE PARTS ARE HER TWO SEX GLANDS, THE OVARIES. THESE MAKE EGGS, WHICH ARE FERTILIZED BY THE MALE'S SPERM.

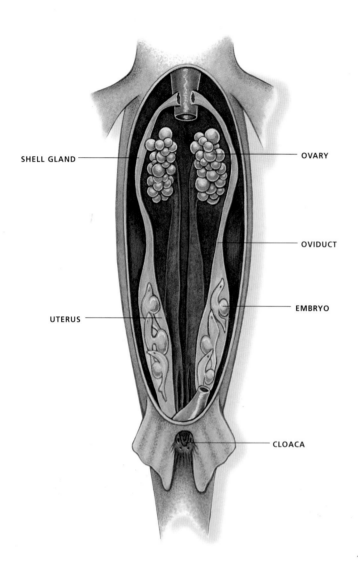

SHELL GLAND

OVARY

OVIDUCT

UTERUS

EMBRYO

CLOACA

Ovaries, like testes, are part of the hormonal or endocrine system. They produce sex hormones which stimulate the development of female bodily features. Most obvious on the outside, in most types of sharks, is the female's larger body size compared with males of her species. She may weigh one-quarter as much again as he does. Females also have skin up to three times as thick as the males, perhaps to prevent injuries during the very physical process of mating. The ovarian sex hormones also control mating behavior, and either eggshell production and egg-laying, or the maintenance of pregnancies.

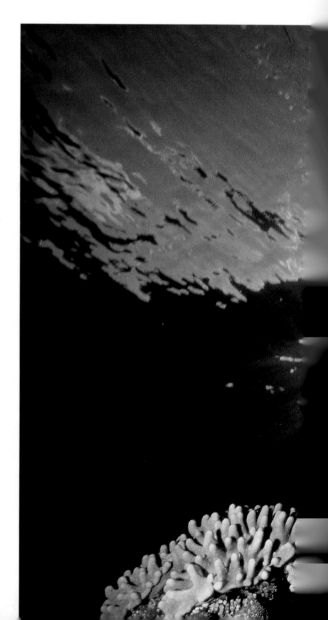

above: **Inside a female shark, the ovaries release eggs into the abdominal cavity. From here, they pass into the open ends of the oviducts (egg tubes).**

In some species, once the egg is fertilized, the eggs are then coated with shells and laid outside the body. In others, the eggs remain inside the female's body until the babies have developed.

Most female sharks have a pair of ovaries, in roughly the same part of the body as the male's testes. But in some species, the female has only one ovary. This is adequate, because the shark's low reproductive rate means that only a few eggs, comparatively speaking, are needed throughout life.

parts of the egg

During the breeding season, the ovaries release several eggs into the general body cavity. These are wafted by microscopic hairlike cilia into the funnel-shaped openings of the two egg tubes, or oviducts. As the eggs move along their oviduct, they pass a gland that makes the egg's "white," an albumin-like substance which coats the egg, and is mainly a reserve of food.

Next, the eggs pass the shell gland, which wraps them in a soft, filmy case, sometimes called a candle.

If mating has been successful, at some stage during the eggs' passage along the oviduct, they meet sperm coming in the other direction, and they are fertilized (see page 172). The sperm may have just been introduced by a recent mating, or the female may have stored it from a mating some days or weeks ago.

What happens next depends on whether the shark is an egg-layer or live-bearer (see pages 174–179).

BIG EGGS

Compared with those of other members of the animal kingdom, shark eggs laid in their cases are large in relation to the mother's body size. For a fairly standard shark, 6½ feet long, the egg in its case may be two to four inches long. Biggest are the cased eggs of the whale shark—as much as a foot in length. In contrast, the eggs of many bony fish are the size of rice grains, pinheads, or even smaller.

left: **A female whitetip shark (lacking claspers) circles coral in the aptly-named Coral Sea.**

above: **A female lemon shark (with hitchiking remora) prepares to give birth in a sandy lagoon.**

Courting Sharks

SHARKS ARE POOR PARENTS. THEY DO NOT SHOW ANY PARENTAL BEHAVIOR, CARING FOR AND

PROTECTING THE YOUNG—INDEED, THEY ARE JUST AS LIKELY TO EAT THEIR OWN OFFSPRING.

A female and male shark have no need to form a lasting pair-bond. They come together only to mate, with courtship as a prelude.

Little is known of the natural courtship behavior of sharks. In the wild, human observers may disturb or distract, while even in the best-equipped aquaria, the surroundings are relatively unnatural, and sharks seem somewhat reluctant to mate. Courtship in animals, as far as we know, does not have the human connotations of love and romance. It is simply a

left: **Whitetip reef sharks gather in their traditional mating place—a lagoon in the Galapagos Islands.**

above: **After the physically robust process of mating, this whitetip shows scars around her gills.**

way of ensuring that animals of the same species and maturity, but different sexes, come together in the same place at the right time. It serves to stimulate the reproductive organs, so eggs and sperm are ripe and available. It also allows each shark to assess and select a fit, strong, healthy partner, thereby increasing the chances of fit, strong, healthy offspring.

In most species, courting behavior begins with a seasonal migration. Since sharks tend to live alone or in single-sex groups, the first stage is getting both sexes together, rather than relying on a very rare, chance encounter in the open ocean with a willing member of the opposite sex.

forbidden feeding

When sharks arrive at the traditional mating grounds, the males begin a fast which can last days, even weeks. This may help to prevent the male's aggressive mating behavior from turning into a feeding frenzy, where the female is the main course! The fast, together with the excesses of courtship and mating leaves them somewhat weakened, with severely depleted reserves of oil in their livers.

Courtship probably involves all the shark's sensory equipment—especially smell, sight, and touch. As females arrive and reach a state of sexual readiness, they probably release substances called pheromones into the water. These are chemical messengers and they stimulate males, who rapidly congregate around the females, chasing and touching them, and prodding and pushing against them with increasing force. This stage may last from an hour or two in some species, to days in others.

The most aroused male sharks begin to mouth and nibble the females. Gradually a male gains the attention of one particular partner, and inflicts skin wounds or "love bites" on her with his teeth. The female may initially resist these attentions, but she then becomes subdued, and has a generally passive role in the mating procedure.

The male continues to shove and bite and writhe about the female, with greater violence. Finally he grabs one of her pectoral fins in his teeth. This is the usual position for actual copulation to commence. By now, his claspers are engorged and erect, and she is ready to allow him to mate.

How Sharks Mate

MANY OCEAN ANIMALS, FROM SEA URCHIN TO SALMON, HAVE EXTERNAL FERTILIZATION. EGGS AND SPERM ARE CAST INTO THE WATER, AND THE JOINING OF ONE EGG WITH ONE SPERM—FERTILIZATION—IS LEFT TO CHANCE.

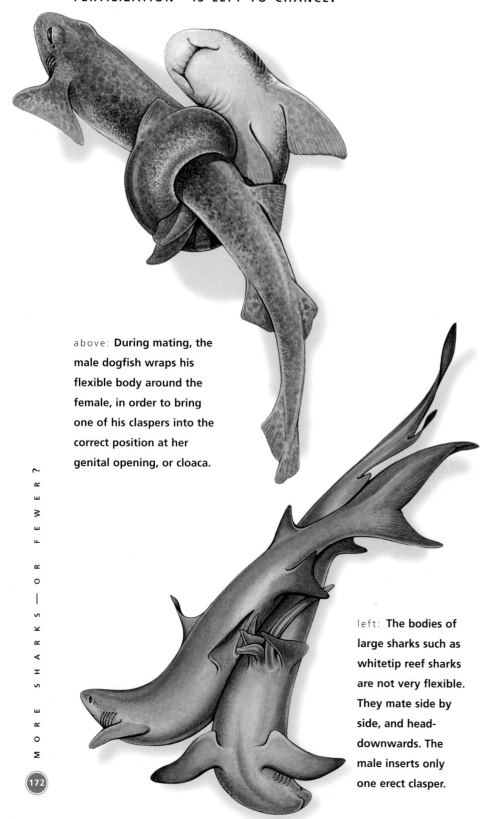

above: **During mating, the male dogfish wraps his flexible body around the female, in order to bring one of his claspers into the correct position at her genital opening, or cloaca.**

left: **The bodies of large sharks such as whitetip reef sharks are not very flexible. They mate side by side, and head-downwards. The male inserts only one erect clasper.**

Ferilization in all sharks is internal, taking place in the egg tubes or oviducts of the female. This requires mating. Once the male shark has hold of a female, he must maneuver his body into such a position that he can introduce his clasper, along which the sperm pass, into her vent (the slit that opens into the cloaca). In most observed matings, only one clasper is used, usually the right one. In some species the male may use both, either at the same time or, as in horn sharks, one after the other.

A small and flexible male shark, such as dogfish, gets into position by wrapping his body right around the rear end of the female. The male horn shark grasps the pectoral fin of his partner and twists his tail over her back, pressing on to the second dorsal fin, to bring his claspers into position. Larger, more rigid-bodied species, such as white-tip reef sharks, may swim head down with undersides together or side by side. Lemon sharks mate while they are slowly swimming, with the rear parts of their bodies touching, but their heads apart.

seawater flush

Once the pair have achieved their mating position, the male releases his packets of sperm—spermatophores—from their storage chambers (the two seminal vesicles), into his cloaca. From here, they pass into the apopyle of the clasper (see page 166). Seawater is sucked into his siphon sacs, under the skin nearby, and then pumped through the groove along the middle of the clasper. This washes and flushes the spermatophores along the clasper, out the end and directly into the female's cloaca. From here, they pass into the oviducts, to fertilize the eggs, or are stored for fertilization in the future.

Matings that have been observed have taken around half an hour. During this time, the male's rear body moves rhythmically against the female. She stays passive until the male withdraws his clasper, and then without ceremony, the pair separate. It is not clear if a female mates with more than one male, or if a male copulates with more than one female.

After the mating season, egg-laying females swim to their traditional nursery areas, while the pregnant live-bearing females resume their normal feeding. The males are by now thin and weak after mating, with their genital areas swollen and bleeding. They also leave the area quickly, to avoid becoming prey to any remaining females.

above: **Most bony fish, like these brown trout, expel eggs (roe) and sperm (milt) into the water, so that fertilization is external to the mother's body.**

Egg-laying Sharks

AMONG THE SHARKS THAT LAY EGGS ARE DOGFISH, HORN SHARKS, CATSHARKS, CARPET SHARKS, AND SWELL SHARKS.

The egg-laying method of breeding is extremely common among sea animals, as well as amphibians and birds, and is called oviparity. Inside their egg cases, the developing embryo sharks have ample food in the form of the yolk store, to grow to a size at which they have a good chance of survival.

The fertilized eggs pass out of the female shark's body via the cloaca and vent. On contact with sea water, the shell material hardens into a tough protective coat.

Female sharks do not always lay their eggs directly after they mate. Horn sharks, for example, produce their eggs two at a time, every week or so, over a two-month period. This allows the mother time for building up enough reserves to fill each six-inch-long egg with albumin and rich, nourishing yolk for the embryo's growth. She stores the male's sperm for ferilization during this time. Lesser spotted dogfish females mate in the autumn, then take the following winter and spring to ripen and lay just 20 eggs.

carefully laid

Shark mothers lay their eggs very carefully. It takes as long as two hours for a horn shark to twist each of her eggs out through the vent. She then reputedly picks up the egg in her mouth and pushes it into a crevice in a communal "nest" site. Each egg case has a conical, double-helix thread which causes it to spiral and twist downward, like a woodscrew, wedging it into the sand or between rocks.

Catsharks lay oblong or pillow-shaped eggs with long, curly tendrils at each corner. These tangle around seaweed when freshly laid, and as they harden, the tendrils contract and pull the egg downward, to greater shelter and conceal-

ment within the seaweed fronds. The tendrils hold the egg fast while the embryo develops inside. Such empty egg cases are often washed up on beaches after hatching, and are popularly known as "mermaids' purses."

Zebra shark eggs are similarly equipped with tufts of stiff hairs, for anchorage among weeds and rocks.

Shark eggs must be securely anchored in a safe place, because the babies take between six and ten months to develop before hatching. The time period depends partly on water tempera-

above: **Female oviparous sharks lay eggs equipped with plenty of nourishing yolk and a protective case or shell. However, after seeking a suitable place to lay their eggs, the shark's maternal duties are finished.**

MORE SHARKS—OR FEWER?

174

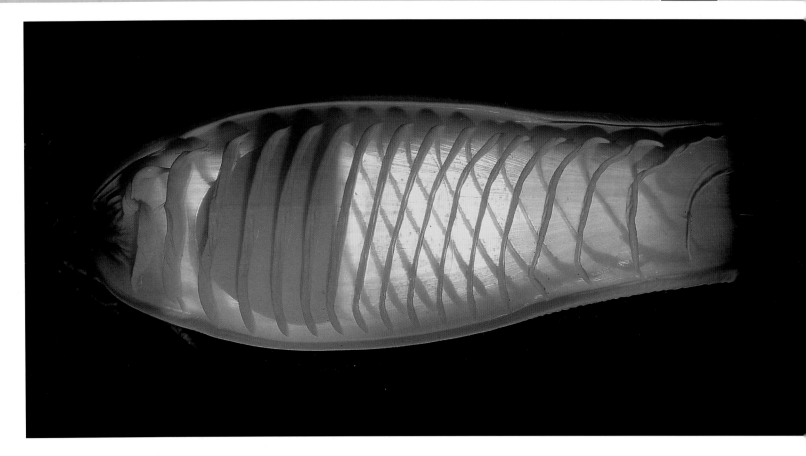

ture. In tropical seas, horn shark eggs grow fairly quickly and hatch seven months after laying. In cooler Northern Europe waters, lesser spotted dogfish eggs take nine months to mature and hatch. Baby sharks that develop inside their mother's body take even longer (see page 176).

(see page 176)

above: **The beautifully patterned egg case of the draftboard shark, one of the swell sharks, some three weeks after being laid.**

left: **The distinctive spiral-ribbed egg case of the heterodontiforms — the horn or Port Jackson shark group.**

GROWING AND HATCHING

1 The fertilized egg develops into the embryo, which begins as a microscopic speck on the surface of the yolk.

2 The embryo develops its main organs and systems, such as the brain, heart, and guts, and grows larger.

3 The embryo is attached to the membrane of the yolk sac by an umbilical cord containing blood vessels, through which it obtains sustenance from the thick, nutrient-rich yolk.

4 Oxygen passes in through the egg case from the surrounding water, and body wastes seep out.

5 As the baby reaches maturity, it takes on the skin pattern that will best camouflage it when hatched.

6 The baby, known as a pup, begins to wriggle and rotate.

7 Eventually the egg case bursts at one end and the pup pushes itself out, gaining a firm hold against the case with rows of large denticles along its back.

8 Most shark hatchlings are 8–12 inches long. They swim off, fully independent and ready to hunt for themselves.

Developing Inside Mother

IN MOST SPECIES OF SHARKS, THE FEMALES ARE NOT EGG-LAYERS, OR OVIPAROUS.

THEY ARE LIVE-BEARERS, GIVING BIRTH TO WELL-FORMED YOUNG, WHO ARE READY

TO FEND FOR THEMSELVES.

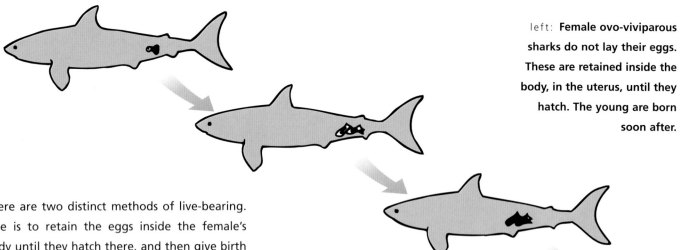

left: **Female ovo-viviparous sharks do not lay their eggs. These are retained inside the body, in the uterus, until they hatch. The young are born soon after.**

There are two distinct methods of live-bearing. One is to retain the eggs inside the female's body until they hatch there, and then give birth to the babies. This is known as ovo-viviparity. A few sharks have the second, more specialized version, viviparity (see page 178).

Most shark species are ovo-viviparous, including frilled sharks, sand sharks, threshers, tigers, nurse sharks, makos, basking sharks, and most of the squaliforms—spiny sharks, lantern sharks, and sleeper, dwarf, and bramble sharks. The eggs are retained in the oviducts and have their flimsy membrane-like coverings, but these never thicken and toughen into proper egg cases, as they do on eggs laid externally.

The embryo sharks live on food supplies in the eggs and develop in exactly the same way as for oviparous sharks, shown on page 174. But they are in a carefully maintained environment, with controlled temperature, plenty of oxygen, and little danger from predators. So their chances of survival are much higher. When their yolky food supply is gone, they finally hatch from their soft membraneous cases and are born (see page 178).

food for the pups

Some shark species take ovo-viviparity a stage further. After hatching, the pups, do not leave

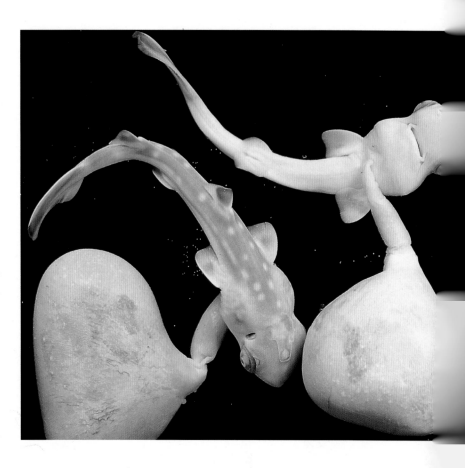

the mother's body straightaway. They stay for hours, even days, within a specialized region of the oviduct, called the uterus. Here, they are provided with extra sustenance. In porbeagles, thresher, and mako sharks, this sustenance takes the form of unfertilized eggs, which the mother continues to produce from her ovaries. The pups devour these as they move along the oviduct. When born, the pups have hugely swollen bellies, full with enough food to last them for several days.

Feeding on other eggs within the mother's body is called oogeny. It was discovered by a biologist, Stewart Springer. He was dissecting a dead female sand tiger shark for research, when he put his hand into the uterus—and was severely bitten by the unborn pups.

opposite below: **The embryos of ovo-viviparous sharks are provided with yolk sacs even though they develop within their mother's uterus.**

below: **Juvenile sharks like these sand sharks (known as gray nurses in Australia) often stay in groups, as safety in numbers from their larger cousins.**

CANNIBALS BEFORE BIRTH!

The pups of sand tiger, mako, porbeagle, and thresher sharks have taken feeding within the uterus to a more extreme level. The first youngsters to hatch there consume not unfertilized eggs but their womb-mate siblings, as these hatch one by one. Finally only one pup survives in each uterus, ready to be born. This macabre practice is called intrauterine cannibalism.

A Shark Is Born

SOME SHARKS ARE VIVIPAROUS. THIS MEANS THE EMBRYO SHARKS DEVELOP INSIDE THE MOTHER, BUT NOT WITHIN EGG CASES, OR NOURISHED BY LARGE RESERVES OF THE NORMAL YOLKY FOOD.

left: **Female viviparous sharks retain their embryos inside the uterus and provide them with nourishment for their development, via a placenta-like organ.**

The developing babies of a viviparous shark live within a enlarged part of the oviduct, called the uterus. In function, this is equivalent to the uterus (womb) in mammals. Within it, the mother provides the babies with nourishment via a specialized nutrient-exchange system, an adaptation of the yolk sac. This is equivalent to the mammal's placenta. In this system, the mother shark, like a mother mammal, can be called "pregnant." Hardly any other groups of animals show such sophisticated viviparity.

Several species of sharks, smooth hounds, bull sharks, hammerheads, and the typical open-ocean, streamlined, fast-swimming, predatory sharks of the requiem group (see page 52) have the viviparous type of reproduction. In very early development, the yolk sac does not fill up with highly nutritious yolk, for the normal egg. Instead it spreads out among outfoldings of the lining in the uterine part of the oviduct. The two sets of foldings stick closely to each other, forming the placenta. Blood vessels from the yolk sac, which are linked to the baby shark's blood system, grow into the uterine tissue, so they lie alongside the mother's blood vessels. Through the very thin membrane separating the mother's blood and baby's blood, nutrients and oxygen pass one way, and wastes the other way.

The embryo is joined to its placenta by an umbilical cord which contains an artery, a vein, and a vitelline (yolk) canal.

the process of birth

When the time of birth approaches, the young move from the uterus, along to the end of the oviduct, then into the cloacal chamber, and

left: **The placenta of this newborn baby dogfish shark will soon detach as the shark begins to wriggle and swim vigorously, to break the umbilical cord.**

finally out through the vent slit, to the outside water. They thrash strongly, stretching and breaking the umbilical cord that still links them to the placenta, which emerges from the mother too, as the afterbirth.

Most shark pups are born tail first but some, like sand tigers, turn around so they can be born head first. Baby hammerheads are also born head first, with their hammer-like head flanges folded back. Spiny dogfish emerge head first too, their dorsal spines capped by gristly knobs. The snout-teeth of young sawsharks are soft and folded flat at their head-first birth.

Remora fish (shark-suckers) usually hang around as the babies emerge. They may approach and break the umbilical cord, and enjoy a meal of the afterbirth.

PREGNANCY TIMES

For both ovo-viviparous and viviparous sharks, the time of gestation or pregnancy is relatively long. This allows the pups to reach a large size and advanced state of development.

• Most shark pregnancies, for instance the sand tiger shark, last about 12 months.

• The female spiny dogfish is pregnant for 20–24 months—one of the longest times for any vertebrate animal.

• Frilled sharks are also thought to have a two-year pregnancy.

• Growth rings on the vertebrae in the spinal columns of basking sharks suggest a pregnancy of perhaps three years, but this is unconfirmed by direct evidence.

above: **Expecting or not? There are few external signs of pregnancy in female sharks like this blacktip reef shark.**

MORE SHARKS — OR FEWER?

Growing Up

SHARK MOTHERS USUALLY LAY THEIR EGGS, OR GIVE BIRTH TO THEIR PUPS, IN SHALLOW-WATER NURSERY AREAS.

Here the young are relatively safe from predators and have ample food supplies such as worms, shellfish, and small fish. During this time, also, the mother fasts—so there is less risk of her consuming her own offspring!

Pups are generally slimmer and more snake-like in shape than their parents. Those that hatch from eggs laid outside the mother's body are usually smaller than those produced by live birth. But, whichever system is used, the mother shows no awareness of her young. She swims away and leaves them to fend for themselves.

Sharks grow slowly (see page 71), feeding on prey that is suited to their size at each stage, which they can easily overpower. The juveniles generally stay in the cover of the weedy or pebbly sea bed, and are usually camouflaged so they can hide successfully, especially from their main potential predators—bigger sharks.

bigger and deeper

Shallow estuaries, coasts, bays, and mangrove swamps are favored sites for shark nurseries. Larger adult sharks rarely come into these areas. As the pups grow, they move by stages, away from the shore into deeper waters, where prey is larger. Their teeth alter, to feed on the bigger meals. Their skin coloration also changes, adapting to camouflage in the new surroundings. And the shape of the body and fins may

below: **A swell shark's egg case or "mermaid's purse" anchored by its tendrils to gorgonian (or horny) coral.**

be modified, away from the slim, flexible, eel-like form of most shark pups, to the body form of the adult.

For their size, compared with other animals, sharks take a long time to reach full sexual maturity. Lesser spotted dogfish are ready to mate after about 10 years, when they are around three feet long. The much larger thresher sharks mature at about 14 years, while the spurdog takes approximately 20 years.

READY TO GO

Not all shark pups begin life in relatively safe, sheltered nursery areas; their place of birth depends upon the natural habitat of their parent. Big ocean-going sharks like makos produce youngsters who are already large, strong, and streamlined enough to withstand the perils of the sea and begin hunting straight after birth.

above: **A young coral catshark rests in safety on a reef off Sulawesi, in South-East Asia.**

inset above: **A newborn reef shark gets its first sight, scent, and feel of the outside world— although the onlooker is a rare visitor in its underwater world.**

181

Shark Conservation

SHARKS DO NOT HAVE IMMEDIATE PUBLIC APPEAL.

Conservation campaigns picturing attractive and "cuddly" creatures, such as dolphins, pandas, baby seals, even lion cubs, are designed to arouse public sympathy and support. A similar campaign using the image of a fearsome shark is less likely to succeed! However, the principles are equivalent. Sharks deserve the same consideration and protection as other creatures.

improving the shark's image

Conservation depends heavily on education. True, they are fearsome meat-eaters yet they very rarely attack humans. The same can be said of the tiger—yet there is widespread global support for tiger conservation.

Responsible education at school and college can obviously help, especially in nature, biology, and wildlife topics. All animals should command our respect, as our planet's inhabitants. Television and books can also inform about the shark's fascinating behavior and lifestyle.

safely behind glass

Modern aquaria are contributing enormously to public awareness of water life, and especially the plight of sharks. The spectacular exhibits of giant tanks with walk-through tunnels allow people to stand inches away from one of the most deeply-feared creatures. Most tanks such as this feature a variety of sharks, but particularly the lemon shark, which is relatively easy to keep, yet looks sufficiently big and frightening.

Many exhibits are accompanied by displays, commentaries, and video tapes explaining shark bodies and behavior. The inevitable gift store usually sells a wide range of shark-associated products, from well-informed books to fluffy "cuddly shark" toys. None of these products should have been made as a result of the deliberate death of a real shark.

swimming with sharks

Some people desire to get even closer to sharks. Many tropical holiday resorts now offer wild "shark shows," sometimes called shark rodeos. The willing holidaymakers sign disclaimer forms, wear scuba gear, and head out to the local reef. They are accompanied by guards dressed in chain-mail suits and armed with prods or truncheons.

the shark show

At the reef, the sharks have learned by simple association and habituation, that the noise of the boat engine and the splash of people means food is on the way. The holidaymaker enters the water, usually with large blocks of frozen fish. The "show" continues while the food remains frozen and plentiful, and the sharks pick off pieces with relative predictability. The tourists watch, marvel, and take photographs. Some guards even feed the sharks by hand. But when the blocks disintegrate and the sharks become more aggressive and competitive, the divers are ushered back to the safety of the boat.

above: **Visitors gaze in awe at an aquarium at Darling Harbor, Sydney, Australia.**

opposite: **A shark show in the tropical waters of the Coral Sea.**

MORE SHARKS—OR FEWER?

THE RISE OF ECOTOURISM

The ecotourism industry is worth millions of dollars. The aim is to allow visitors to experience wildlife at close quarters, in the most natural way possible, with minimal impact on the creatures, their ecology, and their habitat. Profits are used to maintain and conserve the animals, plants, and local wild areas, protecting them from intrusion and damage, as well as supporting local eco-friendly employment. At least, this is the theory. Some "eco"-tourism is little more than thinly disguised exploitation for personal gain. In the case of shark shows, more positive signs of a general commitment to ecotourism include local restrictions on sports fishing, scuba diving limited to certain areas only, and souvenirs which are sustainable and educational, rather than trophy-like products such as shark jaws and lumps of coral.

humans equal food

Such dives can certainly help to change the shark's image, but they depend on guides with a thorough understanding of shark behavior, and there are potential problems. The general wild-life of the reef is disrupted and more sharks may be attracted to the area, which is often near a popular beach resort. Some experts suggest that the local sharks could even lose their own natural fear of us, and come to associate humans with food.

THERE ARE MANY WAYS IN WHICH WE CAN HELP TO CONSERVE SHARKS.

They include supporting general wildlife organizations and also specific shark or marine life campaigns.

A big shark that begins to frequent a popular tourist beach can ruin trade and livelihood for many people in the local tourist industry. We can support ongoing research into finding suitable shark deterrents, such as small electrical fields, walls of bubbles, or underwater sounds. We can also work for the increased use of spotter-planes, watch-towers, and shark bars or fences. Many of these warning and protective measures benefit from people who volunteer their time and expertise.

laws and quotas

The official "Red Lists" of threatened world wildlife include the whale and basking sharks and the great white (see IUCN, page 188). Over-fishing is a huge worldwide problem, but governments are slow to issue quotas for low-glamor species such as sharks. By the late 1990s, only the United States, New Zealand, and Australia had introduced specific restrictions on shark fishing and quotas for their catches. The quotas from the United States, issued on April 26, 1993, cover 39 species in the Atlantic. As well as limiting catches, the regulations also banned the removal of shark fins alone.

shark products

In addition to the protection of living sharks, laws can limit, license, or ban trade in their bodies, remains, meat, and other products. Such limitations are incorporated into CITES, the Convention on International Trade in Endangered Species (see page 188).

nets of death

The arguments about drift nets continues. Some conservationists want them banned altogether, but some countries rely heavily on the income generated by tuna fishing, an industry which employs and feeds many tens of thousands of people. Safer nets and better-enforced regulations are two positive options.

marine parks and sanctuaries

Sharks and other sea life can benefit greatly from the establishment of marine reserves, parks, and sanctuaries. These are being set up around the world, often in conjunction with

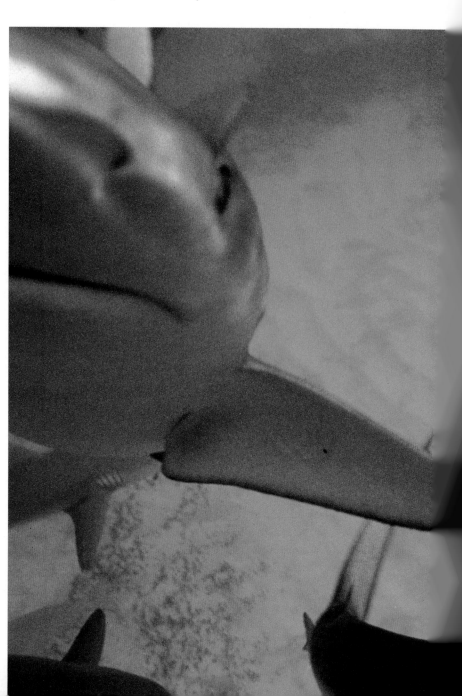

below: **A school of Galapagos sharks swimming in the tropical waters of the Pacific Ocean off the coast of Australia.**

MORE SHARKS—OR FEWER?

ecotourism initiatives. But protecting sharks in one area will not help, if they regularly travel or migrate to another locality where they are at risk. This shows the tremendous need for more research into sharks, and a better understanding of their biology, behavior, and ecology.

Some people may think that the world would be a better place without sharks. But surely these superb creatures, so perfectly designed for their lives as the sea's top predators, have every right to exist.

THE BRAVADO OF SHARK SCARS

At Recife, in Brazil, surfers had enjoyed the beach and waves with few problems since the 1970s. In 1989, a new port was opened nearby. By 1992, the number of shark attacks on surfers was rising dramatically. Why? Scientists discovered that bull sharks and tiger sharks were following ships towards the port, and scavenging on the food leftovers and trash thrown overboard.

So surfing times and areas were restricted in the Recife area. Regulations about the disposal of garbage overboard were tightened. Yet the attacks continued. Why? Further research showed that some young surfers actually went out of their way to tempt sharks deliberately, into biting. The surfers regarded being the victim of a shark attack as a status symbol, and the resulting wound and scar as a trophy! This sort of bravado is hard to overcome …

Shark Classification

THE MAIN GROUPS, OR ORDERS, OF SHARKS

ARE DETAILED ON PAGES 50–55.

AS DESCRIBED THERE, SHARK TAXONOMY—THE

WAY WE GROUP OR CLASSIFY SHARKS—

IS A HIGHLY DEBATED AND EVOLVING SUBJECT.

THIS SCHEME SHOWS ONE OF THE MAIN

CURRENT SYSTEMS.

KINGDOM ANIMALS

PHYLUM CHORDATES
(possessing a notchord)

SUB-PHYLUM VERTEBRATES
(possessing a backbone)

SUPER-CLASS GNATHOSTOMATA
(jawed vertebrates)

CLASS CHONDRICHTHYES
(cartilaginous skeletons)

SUB-CLASS ELASMOBRANCHS
(ribbon-like gills)

SUPER-ORDER SELACHII OR SELACHIMORPHA
(shark-shaped)
what we know as "sharks"

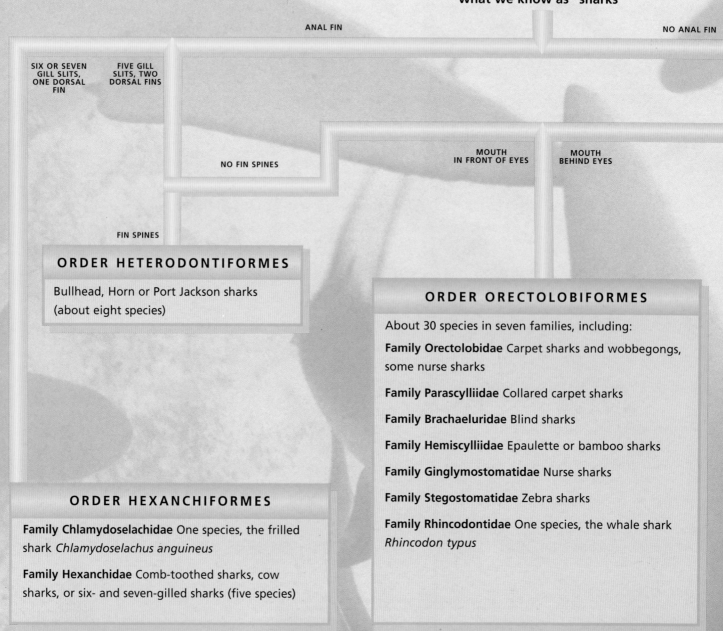

ANAL FIN · NO ANAL FIN

SIX OR SEVEN GILL SLITS, ONE DORSAL FIN · FIVE GILL SLITS, TWO DORSAL FINS

NO FIN SPINES · MOUTH IN FRONT OF EYES · MOUTH BEHIND EYES

FIN SPINES

ORDER HETERODONTIFORMES

Bullhead, Horn or Port Jackson sharks
(about eight species)

ORDER ORECTOLOBIFORMES

About 30 species in seven families, including:

Family Orectolobidae Carpet sharks and wobbegongs, some nurse sharks

Family Parascylliidae Collared carpet sharks

Family Brachaeluridae Blind sharks

Family Hemiscylliidae Epaulette or bamboo sharks

Family Ginglymostomatidae Nurse sharks

Family Stegostomatidae Zebra sharks

Family Rhincodontidae One species, the whale shark *Rhincodon typus*

ORDER HEXANCHIFORMES

Family Chlamydoselachidae One species, the frilled shark *Chlamydoselachus anguineus*

Family Hexanchidae Comb-toothed sharks, cow sharks, or six- and seven-gilled sharks (five species)

FLATTENED BODY

MOUTH AT END OF SNOUT

ORDER SQUATINIFORMES

Angelsharks or monkfish (about 13 species)

LONG SNOUT

ORDER PRISTIOPHORIFORMES

Sawsharks (about five species)

ROUNDED BODY

MOUTH UNDER SNOUT

ORDER SQUALIFORMES

About 80 species in several families, including:

Family Squalidae Spined sharks, spiny dogfish, dogfish sharks, spurdogs, and lantern sharks

Family Scymnorhinidae Spineless dogfish, dwarf sharks, and sleeper sharks

Family Echinorhinidae Bramble sharks

Family Oxynotidae Rough sharks

SHORT SNOUT

NO NICTITATING (third) EYELID

NICTITATING (third) EYELID

ORDER LAMNIFORMES

Typical, true, or mackerel sharks, with some 15 species in seven families:

Family Cetorhinidae One species, the basking shark *Cetorhinus maximus*

Family Lamnidae Great white, mako, and other "typical" mackerel sharks

Family Alopiidae Threshers

Family Pseudocarchariidae Crocodile sharks

Family Mitsukurinidae Goblin sharks

Family Odontaspididae Sand tigers or gray nurse (raggedtooth sharks)

Family Megachasmidae One species, the megamouth shark *Megachasmapelagios*

ORDER CARCHARHINIFORMES

Ground sharks, the most "shark-like" of all sharks, some 200 species

Family Charcharinidae Requiem sharks including tiger sharks, white-tips, black-tips, and blue sharks

Family Sphyrnidae Hammerheads and bonnet sharks

Family Triakidae Hound sharks such as the smooth hound, soupfin or oil shark, leopard shark

Family Leptochariidae Barbeled hound sharks

Family Hemigaleidae Weasel sharks

Family Scyliorhinidae Catsharks, nursehounds, swell sharks, lesser spotted dogfish

Family Proscylliidae Finback cat sharks

Family Pseudotriakidae False cat sharks

Seeing Sharks

PACIFIC

Waikiki Aquarium—*Hawaii*

2777 Kalakaua Avenue

Honolulu HI 96815

Tel: (1) 808 923 9741

Fax: (1) 808 923 1771

http://makaha.mic.hawaii.edu/aquarium/
shark.htm

Shark research program (both field and
captive) with changing display in new 38,000
gallon tank. Exhibited species include blacktip
reef shark, oceanic whitetip shark, and
sandbar shark.

NORTH AMERICA

The Aquarium of Niagara–*Canada*

701 Whirlpool Street

Niagara Falls, NY 14301

Tel: (1) 716 285 3575

Toll-free: 1 800 500 4609

Fax: (1) 716 285 8513

http://www.embark.com/niagara/
aquarium.html

View sharks in a coral reef exhibit also
featuring moray eels, piranha, and brilliantly
colored fish.

Monterey Bay Aquarium—*California*

886 Cannery Row

Monterey CA 93940

Tel: (1) 408 648 4888

http://www.mbayaq.org

Billed as a major attraction featuring "a
million gallon indoor ocean, viewed through
the largest window on earth."

National Aquarium—*Maryland*

501 E. Pratt Street

Baltimore MD 21202-3194

Tel: (1) 410 576 3800

http:// www.aqua.org

Sand tiger, lemon, sand bar, and nurse sharks

encircle visitors in this darkened 225,000
gallon exhibit, part of one of the world's
largest and most modern aquaria.

San Diego Shark Diving Expeditions—*California*

6747 Friar's Road, Suite 112

San Diego CA 92108

Tel: (1) 619 299 8560

Fax: (1) 619 299 1088

http://www.sdsharkdiving.com

Cage diving expeditions where the leader,
wearing a steel suit, baits the sharks to
provide extremely close encounters. Still and
video cameras available to hire. For certified
divers only.

UnderWater World—*Minnesota*

Mall of America, 120 East Broadway

Bloomington MN 55425

Tel: (1) 612 853 0603

http://www.underwaterworld.com

A moving walkway escorts the visitor
through more than 300 feet of crystal clear
tunnel submerged in this huge aquarium,
with sharks circling overhead.

Vancouver Aquarium Marine Science Center–*Canada*

PO Box 3232, (Stanley Park)

Vancouver, British Columbia

Canada V6B 3X8

Tel: (1) 604 659 3474

Fax: (1) 604 659 3515

24-Hour Recorded information

(1) 604 268 9900

http://www.vanaqua.org

Naturalists dive in the tank with six blacktip
reef sharks and communicate their
underwater experiences, through a full face
dive mask, directly to the watching visitors.

CARIBBEAN

The Bahamas Diving Association—*Florida*

PO Box 21707

Ft. Lauderdale FL 33335-1701

Tel: (1) 305 442 7095

Fax: (1) 305 682 8758

http://www.bahamasdiving.com

The Bahamas are known as the shark diving
capital of the world and this association is a
good source of information on the thousands
of shark/diver interactions taking place each
month. Caribbean reef sharks are dominant,
but lemon sharks, bull sharks, and
hammerhead sharks can also be seen.

Nassau Scuba Centre—*Bahamas*

Tel: (1) (242) 362 1964

http://nassau-scuba-centre.com/
shark 1.htm

One of the pioneers in introducing shark
diving to the Bahamas. Offer a shark
awareness program which includes a two
tank shark dive.

UNITED KINGDOM AND EUROPE

Weekend Shark Watch—*Isle of Man*

Tel: (144) 1624 801207

Fax: (144) 1624 801046

E-mail bskshark@enterprise.net

http://www.isle-of-
man.com/interests/shark/holiday.htm

Trips around the island to view basking
sharks and other notable sea life, organized
by The Basking Shark Society. Contact CCS &
Associates on the island.

Sealife Centers

Many aquaria in the various Sealife Centers
around the UK and Europe have sharks of
various types and sizes. The displays and

tours are changed regularly, and there are
extra Sealife Centers in addition to those
listed here. Contact one of these
organizations for further up-to-date
information, or contact the parent company:

Vardon plc

2 St George's Road

Wimbledon, London SW19 4UZ

Tel: (44) 181 971 9720

Fax: (44) 181 946 7353

Belgium

Sealife Centre

Koning Albert 1 Laan 116

8370 Blankenberge

Tel: (32) 50 41 59 53

(32) 50 42 00 2

England

Sealife Centre

Southern Promenade

Hunstanton, Norfolk PE36 5BH

Tel: (44) 148 553 3576

Germany

Sealife Centre

Kur Promenade 5

23669 Timmendorfer, Strand

Tel: (49) 503 352 512

Holland

Sealife Centre

Strandweg 13

2586 JK Den Haag, Scheveningen

Tel: (31) 70 35 42 100

Republic of Ireland

National Sealife Centre

Strand Road, Bray

Tel: (353) 1 286 6939

SOUTH AFRICA

Southcoast Seafari's c.c.—*Gansbaai*

PO Box 638, Gansbaai 7220, SA

Tel: (27) 28 344 1380

Fax: (27) 28 344 1381

e-mail seafaris@iafrica.com

Cage diving expeditions to Dyer Island with the opportunity to view the great white shark.

White Shark Ecoventures—*Cape Town*

PO Box 50325

Waterfront, Cape Town 8002, SA

Tel: (27) 21 419 8204

Fax: (27) 21 419 8205

e.mail sharkeco@iafrica.com

This company offer cage diving and sighting tours from boat decks off Gansbaai (approx. 2 hours drive from Cape Town), they claim a high probability of viewing the great white shark.

JAPAN

Osaka Aquarium 'Kaiyukan'

1-1-10 Kaigandori

Minatoku, Osaka

Tel: (81) 6576 5500

http://www.hitachizosen.co.jp/info/kaiyukan-e.html

A visitor attraction displaying blacktip reef sharks, requiem sharks, Japanese carpet sharks, and 'Kai' the whale shark.

AUSTRALIA

Exmouth Diving Centre—*Western Australia*

Payne Street

Exmouth

Western Australia 6707

Tel: (61) 8 9949 1201

Fax: (61) 8 9949 1201

http://www.exmouthdiving.com.au

Guided whale shark tours (early March to early June) for those who can swim and snorkel, equipment can be hired and snorkel lessons also available. Company promises that in the unlikely event of no whale sharks being seen on the day, a second day will be made available free of charge.

Great Barrier Reef Aquarium—*Queensland*

PO Box 1379, Townsville

Queensland 4810

http://aquarium.gbrmpa.gov.au

Alongside the coral reef exhibition area is a separate large tank of predator exhibits.

Underwater World—*Perth*

PO Box 424, Hillarys

Perth, Western Australia 6025

Tel: (61) 8 9447 7500

Fax: (61) 8 9447 7856

http://www.coralworld.com/sharks

Offers SCUBA divers a 30 minute dive with the opportunity to view over 1000 marine animals, including gray nurse sharks.

Glossary

anal fin fin on the lower rear underside of body, in the midline, often near or behind the pelvic fins.

anatomy structure of a living thing, including the size and shape of its internal parts or organs.

anticoagulant substance that prevents blood coagulating, or thickening into a clot.

artery blood vessel or tube that carries blood away from the heart.

axon long, micro-thin fiber of a nerve cell, which carries nerve signals from one body part to another.

benthic base of a watery habitat, such as a stream bed, lake bed, or sea floor. Compare with pelagic.

bioluminescence production of light by living things, such as glowworms, fireflies, and water-dwellers such as certain squid and fish—including some sharks.

branchial to do with gills, especially the branchial arches—the arch-shaped pieces of cartilage which form the stiff inner frameworks for the gills.

camouflage disguise or concealment, by blending in with the background or certain features of the surroundings, to avoid detection. Both predators and prey use camouflage.

capillary a microscopically narrow blood vessel, where substances such as oxygen and nutrients can pass through the very thin walls, to the surrounding tissues.

carnivore an animal that eats mainly other animals, usually their flesh or meat.

cartilage a lightweight, smooth, slightly soft and pliable, but very strong material, sometimes called gristle. It makes up a shark's skeleton. In our own bodies, cartilage forms the flexible inner parts of the nose and ears.

caudal fin the tail, the two-lobed fin at the rear of the body.

cells microscopic living units that make up organisms such as plants and animals. A shark is made of hundreds of billions of cells, of many kinds, such as muscle cells, nerve cells, blood cells, and so on.

claspers two finger-shaped protrusions on the lower rear underside of a mature male shark. They were named from the mistaken belief that they clasped the female during mating. In fact they act as guides for his sperm fluid.

cloaca body opening used for both excretion of waste materials, and for passage of sexual products such as eggs or sperm.

countershading in animals, having a lighter color or shade on the underside compared to the upper side, to counteract daylight's effect of shining more brightly on the upper side while leaving the underside in shadow. It helps with camouflage.

denticles tiny, tooth-shaped scales. Dermal denticles are the sharp scales on a shark's skin. Much larger, stronger denticles form its teeth.

Glossary

dermis lower or inner layer of skin, below the epidermis. It contains nerve sensors, blood vessels, and other living parts.

detritivore living thing that feeds on detritus—dead plants and animals, carrion, rotting bits and pieces, droppings, excrement, and other natural "wastes".

dorsal fin fin on the upper side of the body, in the midline. Many sharks have more than one dorsal fin, with the largest and foremost one "cutting" the water in typical, seemingly menacing fashion.

ecology scientific study of how plants, animals, and other organisms live and interact with each other, such as being predators, or prey, or competitors, and also how they interact with their non-living surroundings, such as rocks, air, and water.

epidermis upper or outer layer of skin, above the dermis. It is made mainly of dead, hardened cells as a protective covering.

evolution change over time. In nature, living things change or evolve in response to changes in their environment and the living things around them—the process called evolution by natural selection.

food web set of feeding relationships forming a web-like network, showing what eats what. It usually has plants at the bottom, and top predators at the summit, and is a series of simpler food chains linked together.

genes instructions, in the form of the chemical DNA, found in the cells of organisms (living things). They carry information on how the organism should develop and carry out its life processes.

gill feathery, blood-filled body part, specialized to take in or absorb dissolved oxygen from water, in water-dwelling (aquatic) creatures. Sharks and other fish have gills, as do crabs, starfish, and similar animals.

herbivore animal that eats mainly plants.

heterocercal design of tail (caudal fin) where the two lobes are unequal in size. In sharks, the vertebral column extends into the upper lobe, which is larger. Compare with homocercal design.

homeothermic "warm-blooded", more accurately, maintaining a constant body temperature. For example, as the surroundings cool down on a cold evening, a homeothermic animal's body temperature does not, but stays the same. Compare with poikilothermic.

homocercal design of tail (caudal fin) where the two lobes are equal in size. Most bony fish have a homocercal tail. Sharks have a heterocercal design.

immune system parts of the body that work together to protect it against infection by germs, illness, and disease.

lateral line row of sensors along each side of a fish's body, that detect ripples, currents, and similar water movements.

marine living in or associated with the sea.

migration long-distance journeys, usually to find more food or better living conditions. Many migrations are regular, occurring with the seasons of the year.

notochord stiff, rod-like part that runs along the middle of the body in certain animals, such as the eel-like amphioxus. It is thought to be an early stage in the evolution of the vertebral column.

olfactory to do with scents and smells or the sense of smell.

operculum bony plate that covers the gills and gill openings in bony fish. Sharks lack an operculum and so the separate gill slits are visible.

optic to do with eyesight or vision.

osmoregulation regulating or controlling the amounts or concentrations of salts and similar chemicals in body fluids. This is especially important for aquatic living things exposed to low (in fresh water) and high (in salt water) concentrations of salts around them.

paleontology study of fossils and other clues from long ago, to explain how long-extinct animals, plants, and other organisms once lived and evolved.

parasite organism that obtains nourishment or shelter from another living thing, called the host, and causes harm to the host in the process.

pectoral fins paired fins on the lower front sides of the body (see also pelvic fins).

pelagic open water in a watery habitat, such as the open ocean, rather than the bottom or floor below. Compare with benthic.

pelvic fins paired fins on the lower rear of the body (see also pectoral fins).

phoresy natural "hitch-hiking" or "piggy-backing"—saving energy or resources by using another organism for transport.

physiology workings of a living thing, including its body chemistry and functions (see also anatomy).

poikilothermic "cold-blooded", more accurately, being about the same temperature as the surroundings. For example, as the surroundings warm up on a hot sunny day, a poikilothermic animal's body temperature rises by the same amount. Compare with homeothermic.

predator hunting animal that seeks out and feeds on other animals—its prey.

proprioception sense of inner position or posture, where microsensors in the muscles, joints, blood vessels, and other body parts detect their positions and movements.

selachian shark-like, or a member of the general shark group.

squalene ingredient of the oil from a shark's liver, which has many uses in health, medicine, and cosmetics. Not all of its medicinal effects are supported by modern science.

taxonomy scientific study of grouping or classifying living things, according to their similar features and evolutionary relationships.

vein blood vessel or tube that carries blood towards the heart.

vertebrae units that link into the chain-like vertebral or spinal column, the central supporting part of the skeleton of a vertebrate animal. In most vertebrates they are made of bone. In sharks and their kin, vertebrae are made of cartilage.

Index